UFO READING

LIGHT VS. DARKNESS
THE CLASHING VALUES OF THE UNIVERSE

HS Press

UFO READING

LIGHT VS. DARKNESS
THE CLASHING VALUES OF THE UNIVERSE

EL CANTARE
RYUHO OKAWA

HS Press

Copyright © 2025 by Ryuho Okawa
English translation © Happy Science 2025
Original title: *UFO Reading Gekika suru Hikari to Yami no Tatakai*
HS Press is an imprint of IRH Press Co., Ltd.
Tokyo

All rights reserved. Without limiting the rights under copyright reserved above, no part of this publication may be reproduced, stored in, or introduced into a retrieval system, or transmitted, in any form, or by any means (electronic, mechanical, photocopying, recording, or otherwise) without the prior written permission of both the copyright owner and the above publisher of this book.

Cover images © Jamo Images / Shutterstock.com, used under license.
UFO images © Happy Science.

ISBN: 978-4-8233-0454-5

First Edition

The opinions of the space being in this book do not necessarily reflect those of Happy Science Group.
For the mechanism behind spiritual messages, see the end section.

Contents

Preface 17

SPIRITUAL MESSAGES FROM YAIDRON
CHAPTER ONE
Do Venom-like Space People Really Exist?
Yaidron from Planet Elder

Do space creatures that appear in the movie *Venom* exist? ... 26

UFO READING 17
CHAPTER TWO

The Protector of the Savior: A Godzilla-type Space Person
Indra from Planet Energy in the Andromeda Galaxy

Asking about his physical features	30
Their role and the meaning behind the name "Planet Energy"	33
His relationship to Yaidron, Buddha, and Ame-no-Mioya-Gami	36
His favorite food and his form on land	42
Talking about Ame-no-Mioya-Gami's appearance	45
About families and children	48
The reason intimidating security from space is required	49
The significance of using the name "Indra"	53

UFO READING 18
CHAPTER THREE
Wishing for the Resurgence of Earth's Heroes
McCartney from Planet Miguel in Delphinus

What he expects of earthlings 58

A planet that is the root of all martial arts 61

Physical features of his people and names of Miguel-origin celebrities 64

The lifestyle on Planet Miguel 68

Faith and the spirit that space people of Planet Miguel have 70

The God of Planet Miguel 74

The relationship between Planet Miguel and Earth 76

What must be done to do greater work 79

UFO READING 19

CHAPTER FOUR

A Warning about Overwork and Advice on Missionary Work

Space Person from Planet Workthrough
McCartney from Planet Miguel in Delphinus
Goebbels from Planet Engel in Pisces

1 Space People from Planet Workthrough

    Their campaign on Earth 83

    Their physical appearance and their food 86

2 McCartney from Planet Miguel Appears Again

    The reason for the second visit 90

    The reason why Bruce Lee died early 93

    What John Lennon wanted to convey through music 96

    What McCartney from Planet Miguel wants to support 99

3 Goebbels from Planet Engel

Why is the UFO hard to capture on camera?........................ 102

Opinions on Thai Buddhism, faith in the king, and
missionary work in Thailand 107

Recommendations for efficient missionary work 111

The future of Thailand 115

About the UFO and God on Planet Engel 118

The name of the "propaganda minister" of an eco-friendly
movement 121

UFO READING 20
CHAPTER FIVE

Discovering the Roots of Two Japanese Folktales
Eternal Beauty from Planet Orihime in Lyra

The space person's relation to the Tale of Princess Kaguya	126
The shape and passenger capacity of the UFO	128
The roots of the romance of Altair and Vega	132
Her mission of giving eternal love	136
Her physical appearance	140
Teaching about the secret of rejuvenation	142
They appear differently in the eyes of earthlings and non-earthlings	145
The origin of morals in Japanese women	147
Her views on the Shogun's "inner chambers"	150
About eternal love between a man and woman	151

UFO READING 21
CHAPTER SIX
A Space Battle in the Skies of Tokyo
Bazooka from Planet Zeta in the Magellanic Galaxies
Yaidron from Planet Elder

1 Bazooka's Simple Belief: Justice Lies with the Strong

A typical reptilian reappears 159

Bazooka's one-sided view of Master Okawa's dream about
Former President George H.W. Bush 164

Questioning Bazooka's belief as a self-proclaimed
swordsman 167

Asking about Bazooka's superior 170

Bazooka boasting about the dream prophecy 174

2　Yaidron Works to Maintain Peace and Order in the Universe

　　The truth about Master Okawa's dream 178

　　Asking about Bazooka's faction and its leader 182

　　Yaidron is on the lookout in the skies above Tokyo 185

　　The relationship between magic and willpower 189

　　How to develop the ability to use psychic binding and
　　electric shock 190

　　What Yaidron thinks about to maintain safety in the
　　universe 193

　　Romance on Planet Elder 196

　　The battle formation of the UFOs to stand against
　　Bazooka 199

UFO READING 23
CHAPTER SEVEN

Battle of Values in the Universe
Bazooka from Planet Zeta in the Magellanic Galaxies
Yaidron from Planet Elder
Mycenae from Planet Honeykaney in Scorpius

1 Bazooka—The One Who Calls Himself the "Creator of Fear"

    A UFO boldly positioned in front of the Moon 206

    Bazooka's idea of justice and what he believes to be the principles of the universe 209

    Bazooka thinks getting quick results is more important than having love or mercy 214

    An invader's opinion on *The Laws of the Universe–Part 1*... 219

2 Yaidron's Power to Protect the Savior

    The reason for Bazooka's visit 223

    Yaidron's defense power and his physical development 226

    Yaidron's face, weapon, outfit, and skin color 229

    About Yaidron's superpowers and his psychic binding 233

    Yaidron's relationship with Metatron 236

3 Mycenae from Planet Honeykaney in Scorpius

    The space person's relation to Yaidron 239

    Their unique way of thinking about men and women 242

    Their physical features and the shape of their UFO 244

    Important values on Planet Honeykaney 248

    About their clothes, lifespan, and food 250

    Faith on Planet Honeykaney 252

    El Cantare's teachings that are most appealing to them 255

Afterword ... 261

About the Author	265
What Are These Readings Conducted by Master Okawa?	266
Other Books by Ryuho Okawa	268
Who Is El Cantare?	280
About Happy Science	282
Happy Science's English Sutra	284
Memberships	285
Contact Information	286
About HS Press	288

Preface

This is a rare book. It reveals photos and different types of UFOs, and the names and thoughts of the passengers onboard, even though people of today do not believe in the existence of UFOs. Those who have visited Happy Science local branches or shojas (temples) to actually watch the images of the UFOs and listen to the recordings of our conversations with space people will be able to understand the content of this book on a deeper level and with a sense of realism.

Can you believe that there are friends and foes among space people and that UFOs are facing off against each other in the Tokyo skies?

If what is written in this book is all true, we are more advanced than NASA and the Department of Defense of the United States. The Japanese government, mass media, Self-Defense Forces, and space science are all significantly behind in this area. So, I will continue to release information on UFOs regardless of whether people believe them or not. I eventually intend to clarify even the principles of UFO space travel in years to come.

Ryuho Okawa
Master & CEO of Happy Science Group
July 27, 2021

EDITOR'S NOTE

From ancient times, it has been said that enlightened ones like Shakyamuni Buddha were able to freely wield six kinds of superhuman power, which are called the Six Divine Supernatural Powers: astral travel, clairvoyance, clairaudience, mind-reading, fate-reading, and *rojin* (power to surpass worldly desires at will). They are the highest level of spiritual abilities that transcend time and space and allow the user to see through the past, present, and future at will. Master Ryuho Okawa, too, can use these powers on command to conduct various spiritual readings.

To conduct the UFO readings compiled in this book, Master Okawa used the abilities of spiritual speech, spiritual view, time travel reading (seeing the past or future state of the target), remote viewing (seeing the situation of a certain place by sending a part of his spirit body), mind reading (reading the mind and thought of the target, even someone in a remote location), and mutual conversation (speaking the thoughts of various beings with whom we cannot communicate through conventional means).

Ever since Master Ryuho Okawa gave the lecture, "The Opening of the Space Age" at Saitama Super Arena on July

4, 2018 on the occasion of Happy Science Celebration of the Lord's Descent, many UFOs have appeared before him and were recorded as a series of "UFO readings." (As of 2025, 72 sessions of UFO readings have been recorded.)

The UFO readings compiled in this book were recorded between November 7 and December 15 in 2018. We have put together sessions that revealed the truth about the battle of light and darkness that is currently taking place. This is the battle between the values of freedom, democracy, and faith and the values of materialism and communism. We have also compiled sessions that clearly explained the importance of establishing justice on the cosmic scale. All of these readings were conducted by Master Ryuho Okawa, on the spot, when he found the UFOs in the sky.

In addition to the UFO readings in this book, there were many other UFO readings and photos of UFOs that were taken and recorded between November 7 and December 15, 2018. Please see the list on the following page. The ones that are marked with a star (★) are compiled in this book.

List of Spiritual Messages and UFO Readings (November 7 — December 15, 2018)

Date	Title	Book Title
Nov. 7	Spiritual Messages from Yaidron	★Chapter 1 of this book
Nov. 11	UFO Reading 17 (Indra, Yaidron)	★Chapter 2 of this book (Indra) *UFO Reading—Messages from Space Being Yaidron, the Protector of the Savior* (Only available in Japanese) *UFOs Caught on Camera! 2*
Nov. 15	UFO Reading 18 (Yaidron, McCartney)	★Chapter 3 of this book (McCartney) *UFO Reading—Messages from Space Being Yaidron, the Protector of the Savior* (Only available in Japanese) *UFOs Caught on Camera! 2*
Nov. 20	UFO Reading 19 (Space person from Planet Workthrough, McCartney, Goebbels)	★Chapter 4 of this book *UFOs Caught on Camera! 2*
Nov. 20	UFO Photos (Jupiter, Planet Mint, Planet Serpent)	*UFOs Caught on Camera! 2*
Nov. 27	UFO Reading 20 (Eternal Beauty)	★Chapter 5 of this book *UFOs Caught on Camera! 2*
Nov. 27	UFO Photo (Reconnaissance ship from the Moon)	*UFOs Caught on Camera! 2*

Date	Title	Book Title
Dec. 3	UFO Reading 21 (Bazooka, Yaidron)	★Chapter 6 of this book *UFOs Caught on Camera! 2*
Dec. 3	UFO Photos (Yaidron)	*UFOs Caught on Camera! 2*
Dec. 8	UFO Photos (Yaidron)	*UFOs Caught on Camera! 2*
Dec. 13	UFO Reading 22 (Yaidron)	*UFOs Caught on Camera! 2* *UFO Reading—Messages from Space Being Yaidron, the Protector of the Savior* (Only available in Japanese)
Dec. 13	UFO Photos (Yaidron)	*UFOs Caught on Camera! 2*
Dec. 15	UFO Reading 23 (Bazooka, Yaidron, Mycenae)	★Chapter 7 of this book *UFOs Caught on Camera! 2*
Dec. 15	UFO Photos (Bazooka, Yaidron, Mycenae)	*UFOs Caught on Camera! 2*

Interviewers from Happy Science

Shio Okawa
   Aide to Master

The professional title represents the position at the time of the interview.
The other interviewer is symbolized as A.

SPIRITUAL MESSAGES FROM YAIDRON

CHAPTER ONE
Do Venom-like Space People Really Exist?

Yaidron from Planet Elder

November 7, 2018
At Happy Science Special Lecture Hall

Yaidron

A space being and a certified messiah from Planet Elder in the Magellanic Galaxies. He possesses the same powers as the high spirits of the Earth's Spirit World and is the equivalent of the God of Justice. On Planet Elder, Yaidron works as a supreme-level judge and politician and is characterized by justice and judgment. He was once taught by El Cantare on a planet that trains messiahs. He takes on the role of protecting El Cantare, who lives as Ryuho Okawa. Yaidron is an immortal being who has transcended both the physical and spiritual bodies. He is also involved in the rise and fall of civilizations, wars, and catastrophes that take place on Earth.

<Backstory of recording this spiritual message>

This spiritual message was conducted after Master Okawa had watched the movie *Venom* (released in 2018 in the U.S.) to ask Yaidron whether a creature like Venom really exists.

Do space creatures that appear in the movie *Venom* exist?

(Editor's Note: The CD of the Japanese version of *The True Words Spoken By Buddha* is playing in the background.)

YAIDRON This is Yaidron.

INTERVIEWER A (HEREAFTER A) I'm sorry to bother you.

YAIDRON A little while ago, you were outside and...

A Yes, and we talked a little.

YAIDRON We did.

A Yes.

YAIDRON Regarding *Venom*, as I said earlier, no such creature exists in space. The movie depicts a spiritual possession in a way that people can understand. It is a matter of whether the spiritual possession takes over your whole body or whether it stops at the level of affecting your mind. The movie simply uses a space creature to show the difference in the severity of the spiritual possession, so the truth is that there aren't any space beings like the ones that appear in the movie.

Chapter One

The closest beings to Venom that are out there would be the carnivorous space people who are fond of eating people's anima (life energy), like the so-called "reptilians" (reptile-type space people). They exist, but they don't possess people like how a parasite leeches off its host. There aren't the exact same types of aliens as the ones in the movie.

It's true that some types of space people act like parasites and change the tendency of their host to a certain degree, but even so, they don't go as far as to transform the person physically to eat other people. Venom is a little different from the reptilians depicted in your movie, too.

A I see. So then, the movie is depicting a spiritual possession, not space people.

YAIDRON That's right. It's simply the sci-fi version of a horror film.

A That makes sense. We are now studying various space-related materials and were just wondering if beings like Venom really exist.

YAIDRON Of course, if you are possessed by an *ikiryo* (spirit of a living person) or evil spirit and you come to have similar thoughts to those of ogres or devils, you may start doing things you have never done before. There are people who start acting differently. In extreme cases, they might start eating other people or suddenly kill others. It's true that some murders are committed on impulse. Some people may impulsively kill others by picking a fight or accepting the challenge. But even so, I can safely say that creatures that are exactly like the ones in the movie don't exist. Therefore, *Venom* is not the same as your movie, *The Laws of the Universe* (*The Laws of the Universe–Part 1* [Executive producer Ryuho Okawa, released in 2018]), either.

A You mean, Zamza (the reptilian that appears in *The Laws of the Universe–Part 1*) is different from Venom. I see. We'll be careful (not to be confused).

YAIDRON People have an explicit will to do things. When they do good, they have the conscious will to do good, and when they do evil, they have the conscious will to do evil. I'm in a position to give divine punishment, but we are not...

A You're different?

YAIDRON ...we are not the same as Venom, who possesses people like devils. We don't do things like prey on criminals and eat them.

A I see. I understand.

UFO READING 17

CHAPTER TWO

The Protector of the Savior: A Godzilla-type Space Person

Indra from Planet Energy in the Andromeda Galaxy

November 11, 2018
At Happy Science Special Lecture Hall

Asking about his physical features

RYUHO OKAWA Shall we talk to them?

A Yes, let's do that.

RYUHO OKAWA Is it correct to say that you are a space person from Planet Energy?

He (the space person) says, "Yes, that's right."

Can you speak to us spiritually?

SPACE PERSON FROM PLANET ENERGY (HEREAFTER SP) Yes, I can.

A I think this is the first time we've contacted someone from Planet Energy.

SP Is that so?

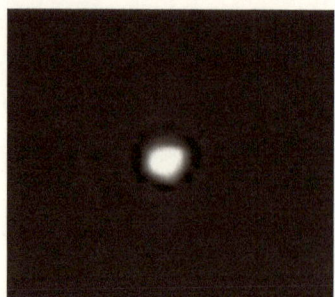

A photo of a UFO that appeared in the Tokyo sky on November 11, 2018.

A Where is your planet located?

SP It's in the Andromeda Galaxy.

A Oh, I see. So you've traveled a long way.

SP I'm on a small spacecraft now, but we've traveled a long way on our mother ship.

A What do you look like?

RYUHO OKAWA What I'm seeing now is a smaller version of the Godzilla statue I saw in front of the theater the other day.

A Godzilla?

RYUHO OKAWA It looks like it, but it's dark green, not black.

A Is it a dinosaur-type space person?

RYUHO OKAWA It seems so. It's standing on two legs.

A Then, it really is Godzilla.

SP Godzilla-type space person. Planet Energy. I've come from the Andromeda Galaxy.

A Is it correct to assume that your people are all Godzilla-type?

RYUHO OKAWA How tall are you?
   He says, "About 2.5 meters (about 8 feet)."

A About 2.5 meters?

RYUHO OKAWA Yes. But they look like Godzilla.

A How many of you are on board?

RYUHO OKAWA He says, "65." That's a lot—surprisingly many.

A It must be a very big UFO.

RYUHO OKAWA Maybe their UFO is quite far from us. Its light seems small, perhaps because it's far away. I thought the UFO would be much smaller. Sixty-five space people on board…

A There are 65 Godzillas, then.

RYUHO OKAWA Given that there are 65 of them who are 2.5 meters tall on board, the ship must be quite big. How big is your ship?

SP For the 65 of us to live our day-to-day life without stress, the ship needs to be at least 80 meters (260 feet) wide, or 80 meters in diameter. The UFO needs to be about 15 meters (50 feet) high.

A Are there both men and women on it?

SP I'm not sure if you can call us men or women. You probably cannot tell the difference. Perhaps it's more like male or female.

Their role and the meaning behind the name "Planet Energy"

A I'm afraid this may sound rude, but based on your appearance, would you be considered a reptilian?

SP We are actually "anti-reptilian creatures."

A Oh, I see. You fight them…

SP I'm hesitant to call ourselves "mankind," but we are vigilant against reptilians... Well, we were made and developed in that way. We are like the police who capture reptilians that do wrong.

A Can we assume that you have a soul?

SP Yes. We do have a soul. Our physical bodies are made from natural materials and artificial alterations. Parts of our bodies have been modified.

A I didn't know such creatures were allowed to be made in the Andromeda Galaxy.

SP We need soldiers for combat. Our bodies aren't strong enough as they are, so we need to make them stronger by modifying them. We are the "X-MEN" of our planet.

A What is your name?

SP This may be a little confusing, but my name is "Indra."

A Indra?

INDRA Yes.

A Are you male?

INDRA Yes, I am.

A Is there any meaning to the name, Planet Energy?

INDRA I simply used a term that you earthlings can understand. Our planet is brimming with energy. It's overflowing with life energy and the energy of activities.

RYUHO OKAWA There's a helicopter flying near the UFO.

A Oh, the UFO is moving downward.

RYUHO OKAWA Is it?

A Yes.

RYUHO OKAWA Oh, it went downward significantly. It's moving a lot. It's about to crash into the helicopter. The helicopter is flying right under it.

What was the name of the space person from Planet Energy?

A Mr. Indra.

RYUHO OKAWA Right. Mr. Indra. When we hear "Indra," we think of...

Isn't the Divine Protector of Buddhism called Indra?

INDRA Have you heard of "Indra's net"? It's a metaphor.

RYUHO OKAWA Yes, that's right. Indra.

INDRA The novelist Kenji Miyazawa also wrote *Indra's Net*.

RYUHO OKAWA Indra is called Sakra in India. So you are the origin of Sakra.

A Mr. Indra, did you come to give us a message today?

INDRA Yes. We are policemen. There are 65 of us and we are increasing our security.

His relationship to Yaidron, Buddha, and Ame-no-Mioya-Gami

A What is your relationship to Mr. Yaidron? Are you one of his allies?

INDRA We cooperate, but he's superior to us. We are soldiers. He is a much superior being.

Chapter Two

A Then, are you a part of the team that is working together with him?

INDRA We were hired.

A I see. I understand. Mr. Yaidron is so cool.

INDRA We're here to deter reptilians and others from launching a sneak attack.
 The name "Indra" is well known, isn't it?

A Yes. It's a name of a god.

INDRA That's right. It is a name of a god. I have appeared under this name before.

A Indra is one of the Devas and is known as the god of lightning, weather, and war. He is a heroic god.

INDRA Yes, that's right.

A So, you are Sakra.

INDRA Are you convinced? I'm Sakra. Sakra used to protect Buddha.

A Right. The name Sakra is particularly well-known in Buddhism.

INDRA Sakra often appeared around Buddha.

A Was it you?

INDRA It was Indra. We, Indra... Well, my name is Indra, but this is a symbolic name.

A Does that mean Indra is the name of your race?

INDRA Yes. I introduce myself as "Indra" because I'm the leader of my race, but we all have the same role.

A Does that mean your people all play the role of God Indra?

INDRA That's right. On the other hand, there are Garudas, who protect Buddha but from the sky. They eat snakes and attack animals on land from the air.

We descend to earth when necessary. If animals like tigers try to attack Buddha while he is in meditation, or when bad people target him, we come down to earth and protect him.

It is us, Indra, who protect Buddha. People of ancient times didn't have any knowledge of space people, so when we appeared, they simply thought of us as "Sakra."

A Do you have any allies on earth?

INDRA We stand out when we walk around, so we don't really... [*laughs*]. We don't appear very often. We only appear when we need to.

A So, you really are watching over us from the sky.

INDRA I believe some people have seen us spiritually. That's how Godzilla was invented.

A Recently, Godzilla has been depicted as a savior-like being (in the movies).

INDRA I know.

A Godzilla beats various monsters for the sake of humans [*laughs*].

INDRA Its original form is Indra, the protector of Buddha. Godzilla is the god who protects Buddha.

A Does that mean you are a close aide of Buddha?

INDRA Yes. Garuda protects him from the sky, and Indra protects him on land.

A I believe the mother planet of God Ame-no-Mioya-Gami is in the Andromeda Galaxy.

INDRA Yes, it is.

A Did you serve him, too?

INDRA Yes. I still serve under him.
   Very few people from the Andromeda Galaxy have been confirmed so far, you know? You've only confirmed three or four types of aliens from there. We are also from that galaxy.

A The Andromeda Galaxy is quite big, isn't it?

INDRA Yes, it is.

A So, there must be a lot of other planets in that galaxy with space people living on them.

INDRA Well, Planet Energy is extremely active.

A Planet Energy, I see. Are your people the only ones living on it?

INDRA As I said, we play the role of the police.

A Then, are there also other races?

INDRA We travel to other planets—the ones which we have "business partnerships" with—and we...

A Guard them?

INDRA Yes. We guard them. We guard other planets.

A Are you guarding El Cantare whenever He is on earth? Did you do this when Shakyamuni Buddha was alive, too?

INDRA We just warped from Shakyamuni Buddha's time and are here now.

A Oh, so you've been involved with Earth from the time of Shakyamuni Buddha and...

INDRA When we leave our planet, we use a wormhole. There are a few wormholes we can use, and we can set our destination to whatever time period we want to visit. So, we set it to Shakyamuni Buddha's time, and once our work there was done, we set the time again, this time to the present.

A I see.

His favorite food and his form on land

INDRA If you have any questions, I'll answer them.

A Is it strange if I ask about food?

INDRA Hmm, well, I don't mind sharing.

A For example?

INDRA Our favorite food is... [*laughs*]. Snakes are our favorite food.

A So, snakes are your enemy.

INDRA Yes. Cobras sometimes protect Buddha, but snakes often bite Buddhist practitioners. So, we prey on them.

A You fight against ferocious snakes that make people suffer.

INDRA That's right. If we're up against a big snake, we choose our fighters accordingly. We are currently 2.5 meters in size because that's the optimal size when we come down to the surface of the Earth. If we become any bigger, we'll be too large.

Chapter Two

A So, you really do come down to the surface.

INDRA Yes, sometimes.

A Even now?

INDRA Yes. I told you we prey on snakes [*smiles wryly*]. No one would get mad at us for eating snakes.

A Do you come down in the form of Godzilla?

INDRA That's a little difficult to explain.

A Do you come down here in invisible mode?

INDRA Well, sometimes we need to arm ourselves more. We look like Godzilla but we are not Godzilla itself; we carry various equipment with us, just like the police officers of a special unit do.

Other than eating snakes, we occasionally help people, too.

A I see. Thank you for doing that.

So, can we assume that Mr. Indra came from Shakyamuni Buddha's time?

INDRA Yes. Although I'm using the name as the representative of my people, we have always watched over Shakyamuni Buddha when he was alive. Indra was always watching over him. We'd sometimes descend to earth, walk around Buddha in a clockwise direction (Parikrama or circumambulation), bow with our hands together, and say, "We thank you, Sacred One." We were guarding him because it was dangerous to train in forests, which he often did, without protection.

A Did you specifically come down to Shakyamuni Buddha's time because you were ordered to do so?

INDRA Hmm. Well, that's because there are extremely important people on earth. They have their own guards on earth but… Well, they probably use their own guards, but even though a great Savior is born now, for example, the police, security police, or defense unit aren't protecting him, are they? So, we are here to make sure no evil beings approach him.

The Savior is currently fighting foreign countries with his words, so we can't have any evil approach him, can we? In case evil beings come, we'll immediately show ourselves all of a sudden. It'll be very quick.

Chapter Two

Talking about Ame-no-Mioya-Gami's appearance

A Have you ever seen Lord Ame-no-Mioya-Gami?

INDRA Yes, but only occasionally.

A What does he look like?

INDRA I said that we are 2.5 meters tall, but Lord Ame-no-Mioya-Gami is 25 meters tall (about 80 feet), so he is very big.

A May I ask you to describe his appearance?

INDRA Hmm. He really looks like an enormous sumo wrestler.

A So, he has a human form.

INDRA Yes. He is like an enormous sumo wrestler and has bold makeup and facial features, much like a *kabuki* actor. He is about 25 meters tall.

A Is he at the origin of traditional Japanese performing arts?

INDRA I believe they all came from him.

A Such as sumo wrestling and...

INDRA Yes.

A *Kabuki* and *Noh* as well?

INDRA Yes. They are like his "followers."

A Then, perhaps, they tried to express Lord Ame-no-Mioya-Gami through performing arts, which continue to this day.

INDRA That's true. Right now, we are in Godzilla form, but...

A Godzilla is very popular in Japan.

INDRA We can transform ourselves into sumo wrestlers as well. That is, if we were to live on Earth.

A I've heard that there are space people that look like bears, leopards, and pigs in the Andromeda Galaxy. Are there other animal-type people, seeing as the Andromeda Galaxy is quite big?

INDRA Well, I think (the souls who were once) bear-type space people also have a strong influence on Japan. I guess Godzilla-type space people are quite rare.

A But some foreigners immediately think of Godzilla when they think of Japan.

INDRA In fact, Godzilla gives people the premonition that a Savior is about to be born. It teaches people that.

A The UFO is on the lower edge of the screen, so let me adjust the camera again.

RYUHO OKAWA It's moving down.

A Yes, it's really moving down.

RYUHO OKAWA It's moving. It's moving because we are talking.

A Let me secure the camera in place.

RYUHO OKAWA OK.

A Can we assume that you're male?

INDRA Yes, that's fine. Perhaps it was disgraceful of us to say that we eat snakes. Maybe I should have said something better...

A No, that's alright. Such information is also important.

About families and children

A Do you have families?

INDRA We do. This is a bit embarrassing, but we are a monogamous race.

A In a Godzilla movie, I think there was a character named Minilla (Godzilla's son).

INDRA Hmm. In the movie, they hatch from eggs, right? But that's not an accurate description. We may look like Godzilla, but we are actually more evolved. We have artificial incubators, so our offspring don't exactly hatch from eggs. We fertilize the ovum, and once it grows bigger, we move it to the artificial incubator, where the baby grows bigger in the water.

A Hmm. Oh, I was right. I looked it up and it's called Minilla.

INDRA Yes, that's right.

A There is another character named Minilla (a small lion) that appears in *Panda Roonda* (a picture book series written by Shio Okawa). We ended up picking the same name.

INDRA That's alright.

A Oh, it's a nice name.
   I see. So, you are a Godzilla-type.

INDRA Yes.

The reason intimidating security from space is required

A Are you mainly guarding Japan now?

INDRA I made my first appearance today. Sakra hadn't appeared until now, right? But if you read the Buddhist scriptures, Sakra appears quite frequently. He appears everywhere.

A This is the first time we've contacted you. Have you been watching over us all these years?

INDRA Ah, yes. But because many space people are watching over you, there's an order as to who will appear next. You have us, Garuda, and also dragons, right?
   The dragons are actually... Well, I said that we eat snakes, but dragons are actually a kind of snake. When snakes gain

enough spiritual powers to join the ranks of gods, they are called "dragons." Spiritual beings called "dragons" exist and they can make their appearance in this world as well. They barely exist on the surface of the Earth anymore, but they exist in space.

Dragons, Garuda, and us. And there are also others called "white tigers." We are all ferocious creatures, but those of us who are given the role of the police understand our place and protect others accordingly.

A I understand. I feel bad for asking you about a different space being, but what kind of position does Mr. Yaidron assume compared to yours? We contact him quite often.

INDRA Let me see. Hmm. He is like the superintendent general (of Japanese police).

A Actually, we can see Mr. Yaidron's UFO here toward the left.

INDRA Yes. Perhaps you should ask him directly later.

A Superintendent general...

INDRA Well, that's how we see him from the standpoint of "police officers." He may appear differently to those in different positions.

Chapter Two

A So, he is El Cantare's, or an important person's...

INDRA He's in charge and is on the lookout now.

A Is it correct to assume that you are part of the group in charge of protecting the gods related to El Cantare?

INDRA Yes, that's right. Although, there are others besides us.

A There are others, but are your people the main force?

INDRA The universe is quite vast, so if you let your guard down, dangerous space people may approach you. That is bad. From our perspective, you sometimes appear as though you want to be abducted. But it would be troublesome if a space person really came and "stole you away." That's why we are keeping watch.

A Something like that can actually happen, then. Do people really get abducted?

INDRA Yes, they do. It's likely to happen if we stand down.

A That's scary.

INDRA We've already identified some cases.

A Are the abductions usually done by the same space people?

INDRA Yes. So, the enemies... Those who you consider enemies have space allies and these allied space people may come to get you.

A Such as those connected to the dark-side universe?

INDRA Yes. These space people also have a deep connection with those who don't want you (Happy Science) to get bigger. So, you need a security guard. Without one, you might be...

A Thank you very much for protecting us. I didn't know that you have always been protecting us.

INDRA You know, we definitely won't allow any Grey aliens to suck you in with a tractor beam.

A That's certainly unacceptable.

INDRA Yes, we won't let it happen. That's why we are stationed in a place where we can keep watch over you, like an intimidating security guard.

A Thank you very much for your holy work.

The significance of using the name "Indra"

RYUHO OKAWA It's moving to the right.

A Oh, yes. It's moving diagonally toward the lower right.

RYUHO OKAWA A space person from Planet Energy. That was a first.

A Yes, it was. He was from the Andromeda Galaxy.

RYUHO OKAWA Yes. We just found another space person from the Andromeda Galaxy.

A That was Mr. Indra from Planet Energy. ...Or Sakra.

RYUHO OKAWA Mr. Indra. The fact that they can use the name "Indra" means they are close to us. Indra is very important in Buddhism.

A They have always been protecting Master Okawa. Their work is very holy, indeed.

RYUHO OKAWA They are protectors. Perhaps Fudo Myoo, or Acala, is another form of Indra. It may be an angry version of Indra.

A That is true. Thank you very much. We really appreciate their work.

RYUHO OKAWA Thank you very much. This was the third UFO that appeared today, wasn't it? There were only two to begin with, but then, this one appeared. The other UFOs are currently... unresponsive.

A There was not a single cloud, but when you came...

RYUHO OKAWA It appeared, didn't it?

A Yes. It appeared and there was a light.

RYUHO OKAWA Right. It suddenly appeared.

A If it were a star, the light would be shining there constantly.

RYUHO OKAWA A light that wasn't there suddenly appeared.

A It appeared out of the blue, so it's very clear that it was a UFO.

Chapter Two

RYUHO OKAWA It must have shown itself. It was under the clouds.

A How wonderful. Thank you very much. This was a precious reading.

RYUHO OKAWA Perhaps we should talk with Mr. Yaidron, too.

A I guess so. (Later, a UFO reading with Yaidron was recorded.)

UFO READING 18

CHAPTER THREE

Wishing for the Resurgence of Earth's Heroes

McCartney from Planet Miguel in Delphinus

November 15, 2018
At Happy Science Special Lecture Hall

What he expects of earthlings

SHIO OKAWA I'm ready.

SPACE PERSON FROM PLANET MIGUEL (HEREAFTER SP) OK. I'm from Planet Miguel in Delphinus.

SHIO OKAWA A space person from Planet Miguel in Delphinus.

SP Yes. I've come from Planet Miguel.

SHIO OKAWA I think we've captured your UFO on our camera once before (refer to *UFOs Caught on Camera!*).

SP Right.

SHIO OKAWA Are you the same person?

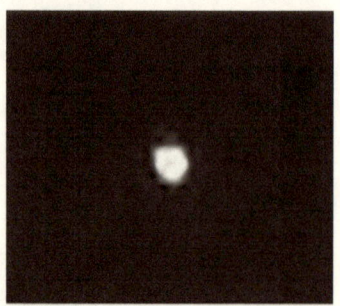

A photo of a UFO that appeared in the Tokyo sky on November 15, 2018.

SP Yes.

SHIO OKAWA Are you a man or a woman?

SP I'm a man.

SHIO OKAWA A man.

SP Yes.

SHIO OKAWA You're here today because you have a message to share, right?

SP Yes. I want heroes… the heroes…

SHIO OKAWA Heroes?

SP Yes. I've come to say that we are waiting for the resurgence of heroes.

SHIO OKAWA You are waiting for the resurgence of heroes?

SP We need heroes. Earth needs heroes right now. True heroes are necessary.

SHIO OKAWA Yes, I agree. What is your name?

SP Me?

SHIO OKAWA Yes.

SP OK... People call me "McCartney."

SHIO OKAWA McCartney? It sounds like the name of a member of the Beatles.

MCCARTNEY You're right.

SHIO OKAWA Do you have any relation to him?

MCCARTNEY Hmm...

SHIO OKAWA [*There is a sound of a helicopter.*] There are many helicopters flying today.

RYUHO OKAWA Yes, there are. The UFO is moving a little.

SHIO OKAWA Mr. McCartney, are you watching Earth closely these days?

MCCARTNEY Yes. We want the heroes to awaken.

SHIO OKAWA You want the heroes to awaken? What kinds of heroes are you expecting?

MCCARTNEY We are waiting for people who can clearly distinguish right from wrong, and who can defeat evil and help others. There must be people like that in various countries. There is a need for heroes. I want to make them stronger.

A planet that is the root of all martial arts

SHIO OKAWA Recently, we've contacted space people who brought potatoes to Earth. They were also from Delphinus.

MCCARTNEY Oh, the "yacon" space people.

SHIO OKAWA Right, right, right. They visited us before. Are you of a different race?

MCCARTNEY Yes. I'm of a different race.

SHIO OKAWA I see. Does your planet nurture heroes?

MCCARTNEY Yes, it does. Our planet is mainly… Well, some planets focus on training the mind, but we focus on physical training in martial arts instead.

SHIO OKAWA Really? I didn't know such a planet existed.

MCCARTNEY Yes. Our planet is the root of all martial arts.

SHIO OKAWA Really?

MCCARTNEY Yes. So, we have almost all martial arts that exist on Earth.

SHIO OKAWA Oh, I see. Do you have both "Eastern" and "Western" martial arts that exist on Earth?

MCCARTNEY Yes. Each country has its own way of fighting, be it in the West, East, Asia, and even in uncivilized regions, and the roots of their fighting styles can all be found on our planet.

SHIO OKAWA Then, do you know Ip Man (Bruce Lee's martial arts grandmaster)?

MCCARTNEY I know Ip Man.

SHIO OKAWA Is (the soul of) Ip Man from Delphinus?

MCCARTNEY Ip Man is... [*laughs*].

SHIO OKAWA [*Laughs.*] So, he's not.

Chapter Three

MCCARTNEY You should ask him, not me. But a hero like him does exist on our planet. All martial arts, including kung-fu, exist here.

SHIO OKAWA Then, does that mean some actors who are good at action scenes are from Delphinus?

MCCARTNEY Ah, yes. I'm sure some are. We are the origin.

SHIO OKAWA Then, are you trying to awaken heroes who would dare to engage in a physical fight, much like the heroes in the movies?

MCCARTNEY Yes, yes, yes. We want to awaken such people.
Physical training is necessary, indeed. Some people only fight intellectually, but in reality, there are times when you have to stand firm and fight strongly.
We are in a time when different kinds of heroes must appear. That's why our planet exists. Planet Miguel is a place where people undergo many types of challenging training in martial arts.

SHIO OKAWA I see.

Physical features of his people and names of Miguel-origin celebrities

SHIO OKAWA Are you humanoid?

MCCARTNEY Hmm, well, basically, we are very close to humans in shape, but we look a little different. It is as if humans had fur...

SHIO OKAWA Humans with fur...

MCCARTNEY Actually, many of us look like humans, only slightly different.

SHIO OKAWA Are there any creatures on Earth that are similar to you?

MCCARTNEY Well... Perhaps we look like mammals with a human-like shape.

SHIO OKAWA Mammals with a human-like shape?

MCCARTNEY Well, there are mammals, other than humans, that can walk on two legs and throw punches [*laughs*].

SHIO OKAWA Are there?

MCCARTNEY Yes, there are.

SHIO OKAWA ...Really?

MCCARTNEY Yes.

SHIO OKAWA For example?

MCCARTNEY Like gorillas.

SHIO OKAWA Oh!

MCCARTNEY Gorillas are one. Kangaroos can also engage in boxing.

SHIO OKAWA Oh, that's right! They do.

MCCARTNEY They're strong.

SHIO OKAWA You can take that kind of form as well, then.

MCCARTNEY Well, these examples may be a little too extreme. We're a little different from them.

In any case, if you train on our planet and your soul incarnates on Earth as an earthling, then you tend to be born as someone with tremendous power.

SHIO OKAWA Are there any famous people who came from your planet?

MCCARTNEY Hmm... Let me see. Bruce Lee was one. He was short-lived, though.

SHIO OKAWA Oh! So, he was from Delphinus.

MCCARTNEY Yes.

SHIO OKAWA I see. That's very easy to understand. I get it. I didn't know that.

MCCARTNEY In Japan... there was an actor who performed sword fighting in Akira Kurosawa's movies.

SHIO OKAWA Toshiro Mifune?

MCCARTNEY Yes, the one called "Worldwide Mifune."

SHIO OKAWA So, (the soul of) Mr. Mifune was from Delphinus.

MCCARTNEY Yes, yes.

SHIO OKAWA Really.

MCCARTNEY His soul was from Delphinus. Yes.

Heroes like him... Well, he was an actor, but we have real martial artists.

SHIO OKAWA I see. Are there women, too?

MCCARTNEY Yes, there are.

SHIO OKAWA So, there are both men and women.

MCCARTNEY There are women as well. Nowadays, there is a high demand for more female heroes, so we're having a hard time raising them.

SHIO OKAWA Is that so?

RYUHO OKAWA It (the UFO) is moving. It's moving in a very far location. It's obvious even by looking at it from below.

SHIO OKAWA We also watch many movies about heroes.

MCCARTNEY Yes, I'm actually willing to invite you all.

SHIO OKAWA Really?

MCCARTNEY Yes. Maybe you need to retrain yourselves.

SHIO OKAWA [*Laughs.*] Sounds like our bodies would be sore.

MCCARTNEY They may get sore.

The lifestyle on Planet Miguel

SHIO OKAWA What do you eat? Do you need to consume protein?

MCCARTNEY [*Laughs.*] Yes. Protein is definitely necessary—without a doubt. We need protein. There is a planet where people consume potatoes as their energy source to fight. But as for us... [*laughs*]. Well, we do have meat. There are many animals on our planet, including the ones we breed and the ones we raise for food. We eat such animals.

SHIO OKAWA I see.
 How many people can board your ship today?

MCCARTNEY It can carry 30 people.

SHIO OKAWA Wow. That's a lot of people. What does your ship look like?

Chapter Three

MCCARTNEY The one we are on today is rhombus-shaped.

SHIO OKAWA I see. Does it only have one floor?

MCCARTNEY It's a rhombus-shaped ship with a top that sticks out. There's a floor on the top part, so the ship has two floors.

SHIO OKAWA Do people of Planet Miguel sleep?

MCCARTNEY Yes, we do. We do sleep.

SHIO OKAWA Are there any striking differences between humans and space people of Planet Miguel?

MCCARTNEY Unlike humans, we need at least three hours of hard martial arts training in a day. Otherwise, our bodies feel dull and heavy.

SHIO OKAWA Everyone?

MCCARTNEY Yes, almost everyone.

SHIO OKAWA I see.

MCCARTNEY We are all muscular. We are "macho."

Faith and the spirit that space people of Planet Miguel have

SHIO OKAWA Do people on Planet Miguel have faith?

MCCARTNEY Of course, we do. We are very polite and we have faith.

SHIO OKAWA That's what I thought. The origin of heroes is God, after all.

MCCARTNEY Right. You like movies about heroes, so we'd like to join you in creating those kinds of movies if there's ever a chance.

SHIO OKAWA Stan Lee (who used to make American hero movies)...

MCCARTNEY Right.

SHIO OKAWA Do you know him?

MCCARTNEY Yes, I do. We actually respected him. It's a shame he passed away. We're hoping Mr. Ryuho Okawa will take over his work. We want him to make movies about heroes.

Chapter Three

SHIO OKAWA How do you learn about good and evil on Planet Miguel?

MCCARTNEY Our basic teaching is to help the weak and crush the strong. We don't like people who are two-faced.

SHIO OKAWA I see. So, you like to fight fair and square.

MCCARTNEY We don't like people who deceive others, who are two-faced, or who try to frame people. We aim to win by fighting fair and square. We seek that kind of strength.

SHIO OKAWA Do you know El Cantare?

MCCARTNEY Of course, we do. We know El Cantare.

SHIO OKAWA Does your faith ultimately lead to El Cantare?

MCCARTNEY Hmm. I guess it does once we "go around." We may be taking the "long way," but it will ultimately lead us to El Cantare.

Many space people are coming to you now because you have many different needs. We are here to help you if you want to be "Superman."

SHIO OKAWA Oh, really. Perhaps we'll need your help, then.

MCCARTNEY If you receive our guiding light, you'll most certainly experience a revival and gain strength. Now that Stan Lee has passed away, I hope you'll work hard to fill his place. You should aspire to be heroes if you want to make movies about them.

SHIO OKAWA Are there any people on Earth who you find interesting?

MCCARTNEY Let me see... Mr. Putin has trained his mental strength by practicing judo and is using that strength in politics; he is using both "ground techniques" (secret maneuver behind the scenes) and "standing techniques" (standard tactics). He's a politician with a judo spirit and is still working hard, so I'd like to open up a path for him, personally.

SHIO OKAWA So, you have judo and kendo, as well?

MCCARTNEY Yes, we do.

SHIO OKAWA Do you have these in Delphinus, too?

MCCARTNEY Yes.

SHIO OKAWA Wow.

MCCARTNEY We have both. We have most of the martial arts.

SHIO OKAWA The spirit of martial arts is...

MCCARTNEY What?

SHIO OKAWA The spirit of martial arts.

MCCARTNEY Well, it's fair... How do I put it? It's "fairness."

SHIO OKAWA All martial arts teach respect and courtesy.

MCCARTNEY Yes. We have events similar to the Olympic Games.

SHIO OKAWA Here, the Tokyo Olympics is coming up [at the time of the recording].

MCCARTNEY Right. We have similar events. We guide some athletes who participate in them by giving them inspiration. We sometimes host an "Olympics for Space People" and invite athletes from various planets to the tournament.

SHIO OKAWA So, athletics...

MCCARTNEY If you lump us all in as "athletes," I guess that's right.

SHIO OKAWA But there is spirit in your version of athletics.

MCCARTNEY Yes. Such as the spirit of courtesy and the spirit of selflessness.

SHIO OKAWA I see. Selflessness.

MCCARTNEY Yes. And we also have a strong will to prevent evil from spreading, like you do.

The God of Planet Miguel

SHIO OKAWA Is there God on your planet?

MCCARTNEY Yes. We believe in God. We believe there is God.
 You'd think that the God of Planet Miguel is male, but our God is female.

SHIO OKAWA Oh, really.

MCCARTNEY Yes. It seems so.

Chapter Three

SHIO OKAWA That's amazing.

MCCARTNEY I've heard that our female God has amazing supernatural powers.

SHIO OKAWA Then, can you also train yourselves to gain supernatural powers?

MCCARTNEY Yes. Training our physical bodies and muscles will strengthen our supernatural powers or willpower.

SHIO OKAWA Yes, yes, yes.

MCCARTNEY She possesses "force"—a tremendous force.

SHIO OKAWA Does that mean you cannot meet her often?

MCCARTNEY No, because She is God.

SHIO OKAWA I guess you are right.

MCCARTNEY I cannot meet Her easily, but I've heard there is a Being who is at the source of the spirit of martial arts.

SHIO OKAWA The source of the spirit of martial arts.

MCCARTNEY I'm not sure because I cannot meet Her directly, but we call Her "Nina."

SHIO OKAWA Goddess Nina.

MCCARTNEY Nina is the Goddess of Planet Miguel. I've heard that She loves martial arts. She loves the spirit of martial arts and of the Olympics.

SHIO OKAWA Oh, the origin of the Olympics was in Greece.

MCCARTNEY Right, right, right. We are involved in such things.

SHIO OKAWA You mean, you're involved in its origin. I see. That's interesting.

The relationship between Planet Miguel and Earth

SHIO OKAWA By the way, how big is your body?

MCCARTNEY I'm about 2.3 meters tall (about 7.5 feet).

SHIO OKAWA Oh, so you are quite big.

Chapter Three

MCCARTNEY I weigh about 120 kilograms (265 pounds).

SHIO OKAWA You are big.

MCCARTNEY I can fight a professional wrestler with this physique.

SHIO OKAWA I see. Given that you have the spirit of martial arts, or Bushido, you probably have a close affinity to Japan. Is that true?

MCCARTNEY Yes. We are closely involved with Japan. Japanese Bushido carries our spirit.

SHIO OKAWA Right. It has spirit.

MCCARTNEY Yes. So, there should be some Japanese people who have originally come from our planet.

SHIO OKAWA I see. Interesting.
  In the past, we contacted space people from Planet Armonite, the ones who became the model for Superman. Do you have any interactions with them?

MCCARTNEY We sometimes meet up on Earth. We occasionally interact with those who aren't our enemies.

SHIO OKAWA Are there any planets with which you have a close relationship?

MCCARTNEY We are sort of "stationed" on Earth.

SHIO OKAWA Oh, is that so! Are you always in the skies around Earth?

MCCARTNEY During our term, yes.

SHIO OKAWA Oh, I see.

MCCARTNEY Yes.

SHIO OKAWA So, during your term, you work to guide Earth or make us stronger.

MCCARTNEY Yes, that's right. We look hard for people who have athletic potential or who can be models for heroes, and train them. We serve as "guiding gods."

Chapter Three

What must be done to do greater work

SHIO OKAWA Lastly, if you have any messages you'd like to share, please tell us.

MCCARTNEY Well, it's important to take care of your body, but you need to be stronger to do greater work. So, let's work together to become stronger, little by little.

SHIO OKAWA Oh, are you talking about us, personally?

MCCARTNEY Yes, yes.

SHIO OKAWA I understand.

MCCARTNEY Walking can make you stronger, but that is not enough. You have to be able to practice your kendo swings even when you get older. Some people can continue doing so even when they're 80 or 90 years old. Without muscular strength, your willpower will wane.

Being susceptible to evil spirits or *ikiryo* (living spirits) is a sign that your body has weakened. You need enough power to ward them off, which comes from muscular strength. The "force" that comes from muscular strength is the power to repel *ikiryo* and evil spirits. Being bothered by many *ikiryo* means that your body has weakened. If your body is strong, you can instantly repel them. They won't approach you if they think they cannot beat you.

It's important to be studious and to cultivate yourself spiritually, but that is not enough. Although it's challenging, you should train both your mind and body to be truly strong.

SHIO OKAWA Then, will you give us your support in that regard?

MCCARTNEY Yes.

SHIO OKAWA Thank you very much.

MCCARTNEY If you wish strongly in your mind, I'm sure you can be that way.

SHIO OKAWA I understand. We appreciate your continued support. Thank you very much.

UFO READING 19

CHAPTER FOUR

A Warning about Overwork and Advice on Missionary Work

Space Person from Planet Workthrough

McCartney from Planet Miguel in Delphinus

Goebbels from Planet Engel in Pisces

November 20, 2018
At Happy Science Special Lecture Hall

Space People from Planet Engel in Pisces

On Earth, they have an influence over Europe. They teach people of modern civilization about the importance of frugal life and provide guidance on living an eco-friendly lifestyle. They look like a combination of a goat and a crawfish.

Chapter Four

1

Space People from Planet Workthrough

Their campaign on Earth

RYUHO OKAWA OK. Who... Who is there? It'd be nice if you could respond to us briefly. I don't think it's anyone with "tron" in their name.

[*About 10 seconds of silence*]

The space person is saying something like, "Planet Workthrough" [*laughs*].

SHIO OKAWA Planet Workthrough?

RYUHO OKAWA It sounds like two English words put together [*laughs*].

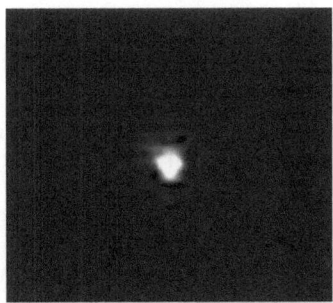

A photo of a UFO that appeared in the Tokyo sky on November 20, 2018.

SHIO OKAWA "Work" and "through" [*laughs*]?

RYUHO OKAWA Yes. I wonder if "Workthrough" means to "slack off" (in Japanese). "Workthrough."

SHIO OKAWA Oh, is that what it means?

RYUHO OKAWA Oh, it's moving up and down.

SHIO OKAWA The UFO seems to be moving.

RYUHO OKAWA It's moving up and down.

The space person says "Planet Workthrough," but maybe it's a "planet for lazy people." I wonder what it is.

We are hearing "Planet Workthrough" for the first time. Is there anything you want to say?

Mr. Space-Person-from-Planet-Workthrough. What are you exactly?

SPACE PERSON FROM PLANET WORKTHROUGH (HEREAFTER SP) We are running a campaign to warn people about overwork.

SHIO OKAWA Oh. A campaign to warn people about overwork?

SP We are working to increase the number of vacation days mainly in developed countries.

SHIO OKAWA What!?

RYUHO OKAWA Is that true? [*Laughs.*] I can't believe it. Although, Japan is doing the same, too.

SHIO OKAWA Which planet are you providing guidance from? Planet Workthrough?

SP Planet Workthrough.

SHIO OKAWA Really? [*Laughs.*]

RYUHO OKAWA Well... [*laughs*]. It sounds like two English words were put together.

SHIO OKAWA You mean it becomes that way when your planet's name is translated into Earth's language.

RYUHO OKAWA Right.

SHIO OKAWA Is that your name on Earth?

RYUHO OKAWA The space person says, "If we express it as 'Planet Workthrough,' I thought you would be able to understand. Otherwise, earthlings won't be able to understand."

What they are saying is true. But their work here might end very quickly.

OK. Do you have anything you want to say?

SP Well... Take it easy at work. Everyone should live a slow but affluent life.

SHIO OKAWA [*Smiles wryly.*] I see.

RYUHO OKAWA I appreciate your message, but I'm not sure if we should support that idea.

Their physical appearance and their food

SHIO OKAWA By the way, what do you look like?

RYUHO OKAWA What kind of appearance do you have?

SP OK. We are always sleeping sideways on one elbow.

SHIO OKAWA Are you humanoid?

RYUHO OKAWA Umm, they look similar but a little different. They look like humans but there are some loose... how should I put it? They are wearing knitted wool-like, long-sleeved clothing.

SHIO OKAWA I see. The ones that are fluffy.

RYUHO OKAWA They are wearing soft, fluffy loungewear and are lying down sideways on the couch on one elbow. I can see round horns on their heads, like the ones that sheep have. Their round horns don't seem fitting for combat.

SHIO OKAWA But they are not sheep?

RYUHO OKAWA Their faces look human.

SHIO OKAWA I see.

RYUHO OKAWA Yes. I wonder what they do to put food on the table.

SHIO OKAWA Their work is probably to support the campaign to take more days off.

SP That's right.

RYUHO OKAWA The space person from Planet Workthrough says they are herbivorous. They are vegetarian.

SP Yeah, we are vegetarian.

SHIO OKAWA I see.

SP Carnivores like combat and will fight, so they tend to make the world a tough place. That's why we are carrying out the "herbivorous movement."

SHIO OKAWA I see.
We can barely see their UFO on camera now.

RYUHO OKAWA OK. Then, let's keep it short. Are there any other questions? The UFO is starting to hide. It's hiding behind the trees.

SHIO OKAWA I'm sorry. Perhaps it wasn't being captured clearly.

RYUHO OKAWA Space people from Planet Workthrough, space people from Planet Workthrough... [*Laughs.*] They "passed through" us.

SHIO OKAWA Then let's end it here.

Chapter Four

RYUHO OKAWA OK.

SHIO OKAWA I'm sorry about that.

2

McCartney from Planet Miguel Appears Again

The reason for the second visit

RYUHO OKAWA Oh? The space person says, "Miguel." Isn't "Miguel" the one that came the other day?

SHIO OKAWA Miguel?

RYUHO OKAWA Didn't they come the other day?

SHIO OKAWA Do you mean Planet Miguel?

RYUHO OKAWA Yes, Planet Miguel.

SHIO OKAWA Right. They came. It's the planet of heroes.

A photo of a UFO that appeared in the Tokyo sky on November 20, 2018.

Chapter Four

RYUHO OKAWA They did. What was the reason they came? I wonder why they're back. Don't they look like they are stationed at the same location as the last time?

SHIO OKAWA It seems so.

RYUHO OKAWA [*About five seconds of silence.*] Miguel... Miguel.

SHIO OKAWA Mr. Miguel was actually "Mr. McCartney" (refer to Chapter 3 of this book).

RYUHO OKAWA Oh, "Mr. McCartney."
  Are you Mr. McCartney?

MCCARTNEY Yes, I am.
  I just want to say that heroes don't only fight. As the name "McCartney" suggests, there are heroes in music, theater, and TV dramas.

SHIO OKAWA Oh, I see.

MCCARTNEY Yes. There are heroes who sing songs or act. We are involved in the arts as well.

SHIO OKAWA I see. Did you come back because you couldn't tell us that the last time?

MCCARTNEY That's right.

I'm from Planet Miguel. Is there anything you want to ask me?

SHIO OKAWA I'm not sure. Last time, you said you were more involved in martial arts.

MCCARTNEY Yes, that's right. I did say we were involved in martial arts... That's because we wanted you to become strong. But after that, Master strained his body, so I felt bad.

SHIO OKAWA [*Laughs.*] That's OK. He's alright.

MCCARTNEY Last time, I strongly encouraged you to train and that's probably why he felt obliged.

SHIO OKAWA Oh, so you were worried. Is that why you came?

MCCARTNEY Yes, that's right. I think I said something like, "You should be strong enough to do *kendo*!" That's why he decided to practice it over the weekend. He seemed to have hurt himself when he pushed himself too much at the end of practice. I felt bad. I'm very sorry for causing you much trouble.

SHIO OKAWA No worries. He was able to rest, which was perfect.

MCCARTNEY Are you sure?

SHIO OKAWA Last week, Master worked very hard, so he needed the rest.

MCCARTNEY I guess physical training isn't enough, after all.

Oh, by the way, an "herbivorous space person" contacted you just a moment ago, didn't he? It probably means that physical training alone isn't enough.

The reason why Bruce Lee died early

SHIO OKAWA There's something I wanted to ask you. When you do martial arts or train your body, injuries happen because you have a physical body.

MCCARTNEY Yes, that's right.

SHIO OKAWA Do you have any means or special techniques to heal the injuries?

MCCARTNEY Well, we have doctors and healers.

SHIO OKAWA Oh, there are people with healing powers on Planet Miguel, then.

MCCARTNEY But even so, injuries don't heal so easily [*laughs*].

SHIO OKAWA Oh, they don't?

MCCARTNEY If you do intense exercise, it will take time for you to recover. It can take half a year or a full year for you to recover from a serious injury. You may sometimes suffer a fracture. You can't avoid injuries especially when you do intense exercise. It cannot be helped. Each person should exercise accordingly.

SHIO OKAWA Even Bruce Lee, for example, who you said came from your planet...

MCCARTNEY He died very young.

SHIO OKAWA Yes, he was quite...

MCCARTNEY I think he was a little past 30 years old.

SHIO OKAWA Yes.

MCCARTNEY He passed away around 32 or 33 years old.

SHIO OKAWA Was it because he overtrained his physical body?

MCCARTNEY Yes, I believe so. If someone had told him to slow down a little, he might have been able to live up to about 60 years old. But he worked too hard because he had some other issues, such as financial problems.

SHIO OKAWA So, you also think that balance is important.

MCCARTNEY Yes, that's right. It's important to both train and rest. It's also important to build your body gradually. Well, you need to take various factors into account, including nutritional intake, building mental strength, and managing your business. In any case, it's hard to do something you are not used to.

It must have been tough for him to star in a movie and run a martial arts studio at the same time.

Athletes tend to be short-lived. But there are times when you need to fight. At such times, you need to train yourself.

SHIO OKAWA I see.

What John Lennon wanted to convey through music

SHIO OKAWA Do you happen to have any connection to the Beatles?

MCCARTNEY [*Laughs.*] I might.

SHIO OKAWA Oh, really?

MCCARTNEY Honestly, yes.

SHIO OKAWA I guess songs can inspire people, too.

MCCARTNEY Right. Singers are also heroes. Heroes are heroes regardless of their field of work.

SHIO OKAWA Music can guide people's minds in a good direction.

MCCARTNEY A friend of mine visits you, right?

SHIO OKAWA Your friend?

MCCARTNEY Yes.

SHIO OKAWA ...Oh! That's right. You mean John Lennon?

MCCARTNEY Yes. (The spirit of) John Lennon is helping you make songs, isn't he?

SHIO OKAWA Yes, he is. Do you know any secrets about him?

MCCARTNEY Maybe it's a good idea to conduct a spiritual reading on him. I shouldn't say too much. You should have him talk about his mission. I'm sure he has a mission you wouldn't expect. (Later, on January 14, 2019, John Lennon's spiritual message was recorded. Refer to *John Lennon's Message from Heaven*.)

SHIO OKAWA Didn't John Lennon say, "We're more popular than Jesus Christ"?

MCCARTNEY Well, that's... I cannot speak about that. You should ask him directly. I'm sure he'll tell you about his music, what he was aiming for through his music, and his philosophy on music.

SHIO OKAWA He had his own philosophy on music, then. I see.

MCCARTNEY It seems like he really had the wish to save people around the world.

SHIO OKAWA So, is it true that he had a message he wanted to convey through his music?

MCCARTNEY Yes. For example, about peace. Peace and salvation were the two messages he truly wanted to convey. Apparently, he wanted to console the people.

SHIO OKAWA Oh. Peace and salvation. I see.

MCCARTNEY Yes, yes, but in a different way (from religion). Well, as surprising as it may be, it is said that there was a comic book writer who was once a savior (in his past life), so the same could happen in music. Once you do an interview with him, it'll make it easier for you to contact him after that. Find the right opportunity. You don't need to rush.

SHIO OKAWA OK.

What McCartney from Planet Miguel wants to support

MCCARTNEY Last week, I pushed you too hard, so this week, I came here to offer my sincere apologies.

SHIO OKAWA Oh, that's why you came. Don't worry about it.

MCCARTNEY Thank you. But I'm sorry. It was really my fault.

SHIO OKAWA Master was having muscle pain, but... [*laughs*].

MCCARTNEY I said that you should be able to do kendo even if you are 80 or 90 years old, so he must have taken it seriously.

SHIO OKAWA But it would be great for us to be strong enough to take a few easy swings.

MCCARTNEY It would be nice if you could regain that much muscular strength, yes.

SHIO OKAWA Yes, it would. We'll aim for it.

MCCARTNEY Currently, he is being careful not to lift heavy things, isn't he? But if he continues to visualize himself getting stronger, I'm sure he'll gradually become strong again. Of course, he won't be able to do martial arts like Bruce Lee, but he can train his body enough to keep fighting his battles for a long time. So, I'd like to support him in that regard.

SHIO OKAWA I see. We, who have physical bodies, must make efforts to...

MCCARTNEY Today is "a battle of messages." While we are focusing on martial arts and aiming to become heroes, the space people from Planet Workthrough are trying to take a nap instead of aiming to become heroes. Today, the dubious "herbivorous" space people also came at the same time as we did, so we are negating each other's messages.

SHIO OKAWA I see. We didn't know that a planet like Planet Workthrough existed.

MCCARTNEY Well, try not to... I think it's actually the mother planet of koalas and the like.

SHIO OKAWA Oh, is that true?

MCCARTNEY Koalas, koalas, and... Hmm... No. I shouldn't say this.

SHIO OKAWA Were you about to say "panda"?

MCCARTNEY Yes, you're right.

SHIO OKAWA [*Laughs.*]

MCCARTNEY I thought of an animal that I shouldn't mention. I decided not to say it. Pandas are "working hard."

SHIO OKAWA [*Laughs.*] I see.

MCCARTNEY Yes.

SHIO OKAWA What about sloths?

MCCARTNEY Huh? No, no, no! Don't make me say anymore.

SHIO OKAWA Is it better for you not to say anymore?

MCCARTNEY I won't say anymore.

SHIO OKAWA OK, I understand.

MCCARTNEY I'm sorry.

SHIO OKAWA Thank you very much.

3

Goebbels from Planet Engel

Why is the UFO hard to capture on camera?

SHIO OKAWA There is a UFO right above us.

RYUHO OKAWA I think it's right above us at about 200 to 300 meters (about 650-980 feet).

SHIO OKAWA I see. Please hold on a moment.

RYUHO OKAWA Is it still not appearing on camera?

SHIO OKAWA Hmm...

RYUHO OKAWA [*About five seconds of silence.*] Huh? Is such a thing possible? I'm hearing a name I once heard in Germany. I think it was in Germany.
　　See there? It's moving from side to side.

SHIO OKAWA Please wait...

RYUHO OKAWA Have you captured it (on camera)?

Chapter Four

SHIO OKAWA Hold on a moment.

RYUHO OKAWA Is it not showing?

SHIO OKAWA What planet is it saying?

RYUHO OKAWA The space person is saying, "Planet Engel."

SHIO OKAWA Planet Engel?

RYUHO OKAWA Have you heard of it?

SHIO OKAWA Oh, it's the...

RYUHO OKAWA In Frankfurt, Germany, right?

SHIO OKAWA Yes. It has something to do with energy...

RYUHO OKAWA Right. I think it was "Planet Engel."

A photo of a UFO that appeared in the Tokyo sky on November 20, 2018.

SHIO OKAWA So today, Planet Engel...

RYUHO OKAWA We've heard of Planet Engel, right?

SHIO OKAWA Yes. It is the same as the one that contacted us in Frankfurt, Germany.

RYUHO OKAWA Right. They contacted us in Frankfurt. We recorded it (their UFO) from the window (of our hotel room).

SHIO OKAWA That's right.

RYUHO OKAWA It was barely...

SHIO OKAWA Energy... They were talking about an eco-friendly approach, right?

RYUHO OKAWA Eco-friendly approach. Right. They said they were promoting an eco-friendly lifestyle, didn't they?

SHIO OKAWA Yes, they did.

RYUHO OKAWA Planet Engel...

SHIO OKAWA Maybe the lights on their UFO are weak because they're trying to be eco-friendly.

RYUHO OKAWA We think the lights on your UFO are weak. Do you have anything to say about that?

SHIO OKAWA The UFO isn't showing up (on my camera).

RYUHO OKAWA You can't see it on camera?

SHIO OKAWA No.

RYUHO OKAWA But the lights are strong in my eyes. They seem quite bright.

SHIO OKAWA But even the stars aren't usually bright enough to be captured on my camera.

RYUHO OKAWA Perhaps the UFO only appears to be brightly lit because it's reflecting the moonlight, then.

SHIO OKAWA Hmm...

RYUHO OKAWA Can you see it now?

SHIO OKAWA No.

RYUHO OKAWA We can see it clearly with our eyes, though.

SHIO OKAWA Yes.

RYUHO OKAWA Perhaps the power of their UFO, itself, is not very strong.

SHIO OKAWA Maybe they are saving too much energy and it's causing their UFO to...

RYUHO OKAWA We are thinking you are trying to be too frugal. Will you make your light brighter?

SHIO OKAWA [*About five seconds of silence.*] Oh, oh. I see it.

RYUHO OKAWA To me, it looks like a double star—with two small lights partly overlapping each other.

SHIO OKAWA One moment. There, I've captured it (on camera).

RYUHO OKAWA You did?

SHIO OKAWA Yes.

RYUHO OKAWA The light seems to be double-layered as if there are two separate lights. It sometimes appears separate.

SHIO OKAWA The light.

RYUHO OKAWA Yes. The light sometimes appears to be separate, like a double star.

Opinions on Thai Buddhism, faith in the king, and missionary work in Thailand

RYUHO OKAWA Space person from Planet Engel. Space Person from Planet Engel... What should we ask them?

SHIO OKAWA Are you the one who contacted us in Frankfurt, Germany?

SPACE PERSON FROM PLANET ENGEL (HEREAFTER SP) Yeah.

SHIO OKAWA Why did you come again today?

SP Today... Well, I came because there's something I want to tell you.

SHIO OKAWA OK.

RYUHO OKAWA What do you want to tell us? What made you come all the way to Japan?

SP [*About five seconds of silence.*] You have an issue with Thailand, don't you?

SHIO OKAWA Yes.

SP It's unfortunate because Thailand is known as "the land of smiles." They want to become more developed, but there's a problem. They have reached a dead end because of their religion.

SHIO OKAWA That's true. They have little freedom of speech and freedom of expression. The people don't seem to have much freedom.

SP I think you can learn something from their situation. For example, they believe they are fighting against atheistic and materialistic communist nations like China, but the truth is that they are teaching the idea of "no more Buddha" based on Theravada Buddhism, right?

SHIO OKAWA Yes, that's right. They say that Buddha will never be reborn.

SP As a result, their king has replaced "God."

SHIO OKAWA Right. Their king is "God."

SP If people criticize their king, they'll be imprisoned. This shows that the king has become God—a living God. So, there are two kinds of faith in that country: corrupted Buddhism and faith in the king—or "living God" who has taken the place of Buddha. They say that they don't need Buddha because the living king has replaced Buddha.

SHIO OKAWA Right.

SP They have altered the teachings to mean that.
So, the reason why I came here is because I wanted to tell you to think about "saving energy."

SHIO OKAWA Saving energy?

SP Yes. You don't need to spend your time and energy on difficult places. You should spread the Truth in places that are worth doing it. How do I put it? You should be more...

SHIO OKAWA Efficient?

SP Yes. That's it. You should think about energy efficiency and do missionary work in places where it's easier to do so. I think you should spread your teachings in that way.

SHIO OKAWA That makes sense. In the current state of Thailand, it seems difficult for our staff at International Headquarters as well as our local believers to do missionary work.

SP Well, it's fine to uphold the spirit of "dying for the Truth," but in reality, it's no good if Master Okawa cannot carry out his activities.

SHIO OKAWA That's right. It's no good.

SP He won't be able to do any work, then. Well, I do think the slogan, "dying for the Truth" itself is good, of course.

It's important for you, disciples, to modestly spread the Truth under the radar and guide people within the limitations, but if Master cannot publish any books in the country, it's basically meaningless to visit there. It is no use going to countries that ban books or don't have freedom of speech, freedom of the press, and freedom of religion. It's better to go to other countries and bring them prosperity first, then influence the people in the countries with little freedom to start a "revolution" there. You can't fight against the military. So, I came here today to suggest you think about "saving energy."

I think it's a kind of attachment. You probably want to save the people, but it is they, themselves, who are content with the current situation. They are content as long as their king serves as "God," right? They believe they are happy if they can maintain the current system, right? People like that can't be saved. I think they are wrong.

If they become a democratic nation, they will face a "permanent revolution"; in a democratic system, it would be like switching kings one after another. The leader is bound to change often in a system like that. But Thailand cannot allow that, can they? To a monarchy, changing the leader would appear as though lower-ranking people are deposing the king, which must not be allowed. That's why they use the military to crush any resistance. They oppress people by using the military and Buddhist precepts, don't they? And they think it's fine as long as they can live off of tourism, right?

But they'll eventually reach a dead end. They have to think about their relationship with China, too, but to be honest, both countries are awful. They are both extreme. Well, I think the Islamic countries will also experience the same problem (as Thailand).

Recommendations for efficient missionary work

SP I'm sorry to say this, but in the end, you will have to think about "saving energy" when doing missionary work. If not, your efforts will be wasted.

SHIO OKAWA I see. Well, it's true that Master doesn't have infinite time because he has a physical body.

SP So, you should focus on the countries where you think there is potential for spreading the Truth. After all, the "80-20 rule" also applies here. The 20 percent of the places will bring you 80 percent of the results. So, you have to choose the 20 percent as the countries to focus your missionary work on. Simply trying to spread the Truth everywhere won't work.

SHIO OKAWA You're right. So, Planet Engel suggests saving energy not only in terms of eco-friendly movement but also...

SP Yes, that's right. In terms of missionary work, too. Missionary work is also about efficiency, or saving energy.

SHIO OKAWA You think about efficiency and saving energy regarding all matters, then.

SP We are carrying out our "missionary work" to save energy.

SHIO OKAWA To increase efficiency and save energy.

SP Yes, exactly. To save energy in various fields. After all, nonnecessities only end up eating resources: human resources, intellectual resources, energy resources, etc... We believe that cutting out nonnecessities in various fields will help society become modernized and futuristic. We think it's important not to invest in wasteful things, or not to use money or people's energy for nonnecessities. This idea is also essential in missionary work. Saving energy is not only important in eco-friendly efforts; it's necessary in missionary work as well.

SHIO OKAWA You mean, your idea can be applied to work?

SP That's right. If you focus on the effective 20 percent, you can cover 80 percent of the whole.

SHIO OKAWA Other countries can certainly learn from the countries that are the 20 percent.

SP Right, right. There is no point in spreading the Truth in countries where you may have to fight against the military. People of such countries need to realize that they will be left behind in the world unless they become more like other countries and change themselves from within.

SHIO OKAWA That's true.

SP Yes. A country where their prime minister must flee abroad is basically no good.

I'm saying this as additional information with the hope that the Happy Science members can understand a little more about international missionary work.

SHIO OKAWA Oh, thank you very much.

SP In Thailand, if you say something that might shake the monarchy, for example, criticizing Theravada Buddhism or the monarchical system, or promoting democracy, you can be confined in prison for 28 years or even 60 years. A country like that is very undeveloped, so you cannot spread the Truth there. You shouldn't put too much effort into doing missionary work there, especially if their citizens are content with the way they are.

SHIO OKAWA That's true. We cannot say anything about freedom, democracy, or faith there.

SP Unless the citizens themselves realize there is something wrong with them, they won't listen to what the foreigners have to say. Nothing will change. If Thailand is the kind of country that removes *The Rebirth of Buddha* from their bookstores, they shouldn't complain about being put on the back burner.

SHIO OKAWA That's true.

SP They aren't happy with Buddha's rebirth, right?

SHIO OKAWA No, they aren't.

SP They don't want to meet Buddha, right?

SHIO OKAWA No, they don't.

SP And they don't want any guidance from the Spirit World either, do they?

SHIO OKAWA Right.

SP Unfortunately, it seems like they have the wrong way of thinking as Buddhists.

The future of Thailand

SHIO OKAWA On top of that, I think the king, himself, clearly expresses the wrong attitude and is trying to build his country based on it.

SP Right? So he, himself, has replaced Buddha. He believes he is already a "living Buddha."

SHIO OKAWA Right.

SP In Thailand, you become Buddha by birth, don't you?

SHIO OKAWA Yes.

SP But that's wrong.

SHIO OKAWA If you criticize the king, you'll immediately be arrested. That makes it impossible for you to do anything.

SP Right? The king believes he can be Buddha because he was born into a line of monarchs. Perhaps he thinks he is God and has surpassed Buddha. That would mean he is even greater than someone who has attained Buddhahood in their lifetime.

SHIO OKAWA Right. According to their teachings, everything has already been decided at birth.

SP Yes. It would mean the kings have already attained Buddhahood in their lifetime. Some Buddhist schools advocate that you can become a buddha by chanting "Namu-myoho-renge-kyo (devoting one's life to the Lotus Sutra)" or "Namu Amida Butsu (Namo Amitabha Buddha)," or by just sitting in meditation. But even so, they undergo some kind of simple training, right? In Thailand, on the other hand, people believe that you can be God if you are born as a king. This idea is similar to the divine right of kings—a concept from 1,000 years ago.

Since Thailand is operating based on such thoughts, you cannot do anything about it. But I think they'll eventually be forced to modernize themselves. It will happen when their economy declines due to natural disasters and other factors, when they fail to maintain a good relationship with the Western world due to their political system, or when they are about to be absorbed by the Communist Bloc.

Unless Thailand gains more economic power, China will... Right now, all the countries that received a loan from China are being forced to give up their properties or land to China, and their economy has been rapidly declining. Thailand may well end up like that.

This is all I wanted to say today.

SHIO OKAWA I see. Well... Yes, I understand.

SP Last time, in Germany, we only talked extensively about Merkel's energy-saving policy and how stingy Germany was about electricity. We didn't talk much about other things at the time.

Well, the EU has their own problems, too.

SHIO OKAWA You aren't only stationed in Germany, are you?

SP No. But we're usually around that area.

SHIO OKAWA Oh, so are you mostly based in Europe?

SP We're mostly in Europe, but now that I have a connection with you, I occasionally come to Japan like I did today. I apologize for bothering you.

About the UFO and God on Planet Engel

SHIO OKAWA Just as Master Okawa said, the UFO appears to have two parts attached to each other.

RYUHO OKAWA That's right.

SHIO OKAWA What kind of UFO is it?

RYUHO OKAWA I can see two parts, the upper one and the lower one. It seems like two parts are attached together.

SHIO OKAWA On the screen, it's blinking a lot.

RYUHO OKAWA With the naked eye, it appears to have two separate parts.

SHIO OKAWA Yes, it does.

SP Right. Well, we are saving energy, so we can't make our light any brighter.

SHIO OKAWA Umm...

SP You want to ask about the shape of our flying saucer?

SHIO OKAWA Yes.

SP Well, it's similar to the shape of a hamburger.

SHIO OKAWA I see. How many people can board your UFO?

SP It's for three people [*laughs*].

SHIO OKAWA Three? [*Laughs.*]

SP Yes. Because we are saving energy.

SHIO OKAWA I see.
By the way, do you worship God on your planet?

SP Hmm... Well, our god... Our planet is "saving energy," so there aren't many people.

SHIO OKAWA Oh, so the population isn't so big to begin with.

SP That's right. There aren't many people, so Almighty God probably isn't here with us. We only have a "branch office" for Him to visit.

SHIO OKAWA The universe is so interesting.

SP Perhaps someone who wouldn't be considered as great on Earth might be serving as "god" on our planet. I don't know the equivalent on Earth... Maybe it might be someone who cannot quite make it into the Tathagata Realm of the eighth dimension. It may be someone from the levels between the eighth and the seventh dimensions, which you call the Brahma Realm. Or they may be a little closer to a bodhisattva.

SHIO OKAWA But on Earth, too, eighth dimensional beings are now considered great.

SP Can they be considered a god?

SHIO OKAWA Well, I don't know if they will continue to be considered a god in the future because beings of even higher dimensions have been revealed recently.

SP In any case, I think our "god" is not in the ninth dimension. We don't have a big population anyway.

SHIO OKAWA I see.
 By the way, are there both men and women on your planet?

SP Yes, there are both sexes.

The name of the "propaganda minister" of an eco-friendly movement

SHIO OKAWA What is your name?

SP Oh, me?

SHIO OKAWA Yes.

SP OK. But revealing my name may pose a problem. It has a bad ring to it.

SHIO OKAWA Is that so?

SP Do you want to know?

SHIO OKAWA If you put it that way...

SP Given that I'm a space person from Planet Engel, hearing my name "Goebbels" offends you, doesn't it?

SHIO OKAWA Goe... [*smiles wryly*]. And you were in Germany.

GOEBBELS Well, it's quite a common name there.

SHIO OKAWA Oh, then, is it correct to understand that you have no relation to Goebbels from Nazi Germany?

GOEBBELS Well, my name is "Goebbels." I'm not the German propaganda minister that people know about, but I'm the "propaganda minister" of eco-friendly movement [*laughs*].

SHIO OKAWA I see. You mean your name just happened to be the same when you translated it into a language on Earth.

GOEBBELS That's right. As the "propaganda minister" of an eco-friendly movement, I am traveling around various places to promote saving energy.

SHIO OKAWA I see, I see. I understand. Don't worry.

GOEBBELS Saving energy. I'm going around telling people to "take the shortcut." I'm not a Nazi, though. Unfortunately, my name happens to sound bad.

SHIO OKAWA OK, OK. You just happened to have the same name.

GOEBBELS I'm sorry. My name ended up like this when I translated it into German.

SHIO OKAWA I see. I understand. Are you the same person we talked to in Frankfurt?

GOEBBELS That's right.

RYUHO OKAWA Looking at the UFO from below, it sometimes looks like a double star. It looks like a star that split.

SHIO OKAWA Master has quite great eyesight. Anyway, thank you very much for today.

GOEBBELS OK. Shall we wrap up here? We have to "save" our energy.

SHIO OKAWA Yes. Thank you very much.

RYUHO OKAWA [*Claps his hands three times.*] OK.

UFO READING 20

CHAPTER FIVE
Discovering the Roots of Two Japanese Folktales

Eternal Beauty from Planet Orihime in Lyra

Recorded on November 27, 2018
At Happy Science Special Lecture Hall

The space person's relation to the Tale of Princess Kaguya

RYUHO OKAWA You there, the one that is shedding an orange light. The one shedding an orange light, are you able to speak? The one with the orange-colored light.

A I'm moving the camera. OK, it's in the camera frame.

RYUHO OKAWA The light is just above the Happy Science local temple.

A Is it?

RYUHO OKAWA I think it is.
 [*To the light*] Is there anything you'd like to say?
 I hear someone saying, "*Nukata-no-Okimi*" (Princess Nukata, a poet from seventh-century Japan).

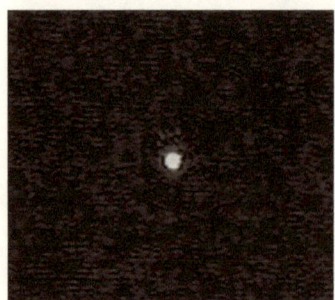

A photo of a UFO that appeared in the Tokyo sky on November 27, 2018.

Chapter Five

A Is Nukata-no-Okimi aboard the ship?

RYUHO OKAWA She shouldn't be in outer space. I wonder what she means.

What do you mean by Nukata-no-Okimi?

She says she has some connection with outer space. Of course, it wouldn't be surprising if she had some connection.

A Do you mean that you are related to the root of (the soul of) Princess Oto-Tachibana (who is said to be the past life of Nukata-no-Okimi)?

NUKATA-NO-OKIMI Yes, that's right.

A Are you female?

NUKATA-NO-OKIMI Yes. I'm the one who is related to the Tale of Princess Kaguya.

A Oh, is that so?

NUKATA-NO-OKIMI Yes.

A Does that mean the story was modeled after you?

NUKATA-NO-OKIMI Yes. That kind of incident happened again and again in the past. There were many accounts of space people coming down from the sky, being raised on earth, and returning to the sky.

The shape and passenger capacity of the UFO

A How many people can board the UFO you are riding in today?

NUKATA-NO-OKIMI Fifty people.

A That's quite a large ship.

RYUHO OKAWA The UFO is swaying from side to side.

A Yes.

RYUHO OKAWA It's swaying from side to side and also up and down. It is wavering and moving both horizontally and vertically.

A A UFO for 50 people?

NUKATA-NO-OKIMI Yes, it's quite big.

Chapter Five

RYUHO OKAWA It's shaking a lot.

A Yes.
Are both men and women aboard?

NUKATA-NO-OKIMI Yes.

A Can you describe the shape of your UFO?

RYUHO OKAWA What does it look like? [*About five seconds of silence.*] She is explaining it in a complicated way. She says it's the shape of a double helix.
   What do you mean by a double helix?

A A double helix...

RYUHO OKAWA What do you mean exactly? We don't understand.

A [*While drawing the shape with her hands.*] Maybe she means like this.

RYUHO OKAWA By a helix, she probably means a shape that is wrapped around like a coil. But what does she mean by a double helix?

A I think she means to say a spiraling staircase...

RYUHO OKAWA She says a "double helix" but is that even possible? What does she mean?

A So, it's not hamburger-shaped. Perhaps it's a bunch of thin, long lines stuck together into a coil-like shape?

RYUHO OKAWA Maybe it looks like a mosquito repellent coil but is oriented vertically. I mean, a coil that has been pulled up at the middle, creating a cone shape.

A Are you saying that it looks like a three-dimensional version of a mosquito repellent coil?

RYUHO OKAWA Do you mean to say that two of these shapes are stuck together? Please explain it to us.

NUKATA-NO-OKIMI [*About 5 seconds of silence.*] Yes. Usually, UFOs look like two bowls joined at the wider side. But ours is in the shape of two bowls put together at the base so that the wider side faces outward. It looks like a spiral. Our UFO has this kind of design.

A Interesting. That's unusual.

RYUHO OKAWA It's a little hard to understand. But I guess it's like sticking the bottoms of the bowls together so that the wider side faces outward. I suppose that's possible. Maybe it's shaped like a bowl on a pottery wheel.

A Is it like the device used to send signals to a satellite?

RYUHO OKAWA It's like the device equipped on satellites.

A There were scenes of a satellite dish in a movie with Wolverine (in *X-men*). Her UFO probably looks like two shells joined back-to-back.

RYUHO OKAWA Two shells joined back-to-back?

A A shell usually looks like this. [*Forms the shape of a closed shell with her hands.*]

RYUHO OKAWA Yes, yes.

A But when you flip the two like this... [*Forms the shape of two shells stuck together on their base with her hands.*]

RYUHO OKAWA Yes, I understand what you are saying. But from what I can see, it's similar to the shape of a satellite dish.

It looks as if two Olympic cauldrons are attached together at the bottom. I suspect that this UFO can rotate freely.

A Oh, how about this? It must look like a *taiko*, or a Japanese *tsuzumi* drum (that has the shape of an hourglass).

RYUHO OKAWA Ah, yes. That's a closer description.

A I see.

RYUHO OKAWA The UFO is now upright, but I think it can also be oriented horizontally. It can probably move in any way it wants.

A Oh, the UFO is going up toward the top of the camera frame.

The roots of the romance of Altair and Vega

A You said you're from a planet with deep relations to Nukata-no-Okimi. What kind of space people are you?

NUKATA-NO-OKIMI In outer space, there is a planet that became the origin of the story of Orihime (weaver princess), who is a character from the Tale of Orihime and Hikoboshi (also known as the romance of Altair and Vega).

Chapter Five

A Are you talking about Vega?

NUKATA-NO-OKIMI The root of Orihime lies near it.

A [*About 20 seconds of silence.*] The root of Orihime?

NUKATA-NO-OKIMI People from Vega don't talk about Orihime, do they?

A No, they don't.

NUKATA-NO-OKIMI But the story of Orihime really exists.

A Do you mean Alpha Lyrae?

NUKATA-NO-OKIMI Well, that's Vega. Alpha Lyrae is Vega.

A So, you aren't talking about that.

NUKATA-NO-OKIMI Well, there are many planets within Lyra. If I were to explain it in detail... hmm, I can only describe my planet as "Planet Orihime" in Earth's language.

In a way, Orihime has some connection with Amaterasu. But Orihime's story in the folktale isn't simply about weaving, as it is in the case of Amaterasu. There is also a promise between Orihime and Hikoboshi that they will meet once a year, isn't there? The meeting takes place on the day of *tanabata* (the Star Festival) on July 7. The story goes that they have a chance to meet each other once a year, which is true; someone really comes from our planet to meet their loved one on Earth once a year. This actually happened in the past.

A Oh, so the original story is about someone coming to Earth?

NUKATA-NO-OKIMI Yes, that's right. It was about someone coming from Planet Orihime. She was a space person who took the form of Orihime and came down to Earth. She lived in this world but returned to the skies with the promise that she would come back once a year, on July 7, to meet her loved one.

Alpha Lyrae is a fixed star, so it's different. We can only describe ours as "Planet Orihime," or Planet of Weavers. There are several stars so...

A In that case, does that mean your planet is also different from the third or fourth planet of Vega?

NUKATA-NO-OKIMI It's different from those two.

A So, like *The Tale of the Bamboo Cutter*...

NUKATA-NO-OKIMI Yes. Many of our people went to Earth and came back to our planet by ascending into the skies, just as the story goes.

A It's very similar to the story of *Tennyo-no-Hagoromo* ("Feather robe of the heavenly maiden").

NUKATA-NO-OKIMI Yes, that's right. It's very similar. Someone from our planet who wore a feather robe went to Earth with others to have fun but was left behind. Their UFO took off without her [*laughs*], so she couldn't go home.

A Was she a friend of yours?

NUKATA-NO-OKIMI Well, you could call her that. There was a time when we were on the same planet.

A Oh, so you lived on the same planet.

NUKATA-NO-OKIMI Uh-huh.

Her mission of giving eternal love

A What are you called in outer space?

NUKATA-NO-OKIMI My name in outer space... Let's see. I believe there are many people who have a similar role to mine so...

A Really? I don't think so.

NUKATA-NO-OKIMI Anyway, I'm a woman who celebrates tanabata (the Star Festival).

A Do you?

NUKATA-NO-OKIMI Uh-huh. I'm a woman who celebrates tanabata. El Cantare was born on July 7 in this lifetime, right? So, Planet Orihime has a deep connection with Him.

A Oh, with El Cantare?

NUKATA-NO-OKIMI That's why I come to see El Cantare on July 7. I come to meet Him.

A You do?

Chapter Five

NUKATA-NO-OKIMI Yes, I come to see Him.

A Wow, how romantic.

NUKATA-NO-OKIMI On July 7, a ladder descends from heaven to earth so that we can come down.
　　In the future, I'm sure July 7 will become a very important day. On that day, you will be able to meet people from outer space.

RYUHO OKAWA Is the UFO moving?

A Yes. I'm adjusting the camera again. There. It's in the camera frame now.

RYUHO OKAWA Good.

NUKATA-NO-OKIMI I'm from Planet Orihime. It's not the third or fourth planet of Vega but a planet located nearby.

A So, you aren't exactly Vegans?

NUKATA-NO-OKIMI You can categorize us as Vegans, but when we appear in front of you, we'll take the form of heavenly maidens.

A Oh, I almost forgot to ask. What's your name?

NUKATA-NO-OKIMI Oh, my name?

A Yes, the name that you use in outer space.

NUKATA-NO-OKIMI My name in outer space... Hmm, my name is... Well, I'd rather not reveal it. It's a bit embarrassing. Isn't Orihime good enough? I'm not sure if I should say my name.

A But Orihime sounds quite vague.

NUKATA-NO-OKIMI Well, my name actually means "eternal lover."

A That's so cool.

NUKATA-NO-OKIMI Hmm, what would the name be if I were to translate "eternal lover" into Earth's language?

A Hmm...

NUKATA-NO-OKIMI "Eternal Beauty."

A I see.

ETERNAL BEAUTY Yes, Eternal Beauty.

A The Japanese woman in connection with your soul appeared in one of the Happy Science movies.

ETERNAL BEAUTY My work is to bring romantic feelings to people on Earth.

A I see. Is that your work, or the mission of your soul?

ETERNAL BEAUTY Yes. My work is to give eternal love to people's hearts. I encourage men and women to unite, not in an animalistic sense but to practice eternal love or love on a higher level. I'm working to light the candle of eternal love within people's hearts.

A Master Okawa watches many movies, and he favors works that make him feel a sense of eternity. This is true even with romantic movies.

ETERNAL BEAUTY We want to be eternal beings. Yes, we want to be that way forever. One of the characteristics of our planet is that we don't age. We are eternally young. That's why no matter how many times we visit Earth, we are always young [*laughs*].

Her physical appearance

A I'm certain that you look very beautiful. Can you tell us more about your appearance, such as your hair color? Are you able to change its color?

ETERNAL BEAUTY We look like the beautiful women from Nara and Heian periods (in the seventh to twelfth centuries), and we wear the feather robes of heavenly maidens.

A Is there a specific color you prefer for your robe, for example?

ETERNAL BEAUTY Well, I wear multiple layers of *kimono* and the inner layer I'm wearing now is very close to the color purple.

A Oh, purple.

ETERNAL BEAUTY And I also wear a *uchikake* (formal outer attire of kimono).
My hair is tied in a bow like the hairstyle of Otohime or the princesses in the *Ryugu-jo* (Dragon Palace).

A In other words, you currently have an Asian-style appearance.

Chapter Five

ETERNAL BEAUTY Yes. I look Asian. I have eternal beauty and will remain beautiful forever.

A I see. Is it correct to assume that you also have relations to Western culture?

ETERNAL BEAUTY Well, there are beautiful women in the West as well, and they will show themselves when necessary. These Western or Scandinavian beauties come from planets different from ours. We are the origin of the folktales of Orihime and Hikoboshi (Altair and Vega), tanabata (star festival), *The Tale of the Bamboo Cutter*, and hagoromo (feather robe). Occasionally, we come down to teach people about eternity before going back. That's our job.

So, July 7 is an important day. I hope more people across Japan will offer prayers on July 7.

A Is the number 7 considered a lucky number on your planet, too?

ETERNAL BEAUTY Yes. You recently saw the number 77 many times, right?

A Yes, we did. We saw the number 7777 several times in a row, such as on license plates.

ETERNAL BEAUTY Yes, you saw it one after the other [*laughs*].

A Oh, was that an inspiration sent by you?

ETERNAL BEAUTY Well, that might've been a coincidence.

A Oh, a coincidence. But it was rather unusual.

Teaching about the secret of rejuvenation

A Is there a reason why you came here today?

ETERNAL BEAUTY Yes, there is, as a matter of fact.

A Let me adjust the camera again. The UFO keeps going up and out of the camera frame.

RYUHO OKAWA Is it moving up?

A Yes. I'm moving the camera. OK, it's set in place.

ETERNAL BEAUTY Master Okawa looks as though he has become younger even though he has aged, doesn't he?

A Yes.

ETERNAL BEAUTY Right? We have something to do with it.

A Oh, thank you very much.

ETERNAL BEAUTY We cast a magic spell on him to become young again.

A We appreciate that.

ETERNAL BEAUTY We are eternal beauty. Yes, eternal beauty.

A I see. I believe men can also emit a beautiful aura from within.

ETERNAL BEAUTY Yes, that's true.

A Are you involved in such matters?

ETERNAL BEAUTY Yes. It's a type of magic. On our planet, the "fountain of rejuvenation," the "apple tree of rejuvenation," and many other things of the sort actually exist [*laughs*].

A We sometimes hear about the story of Yoro Fall in Japanese folktales, where the main character finds sweet water in the mountains that can make people young again. Does such water really exist?

ETERNAL BEAUTY On our planet, it does. Maybe in the past, someone flew to our planet in a UFO and came back to Earth after having such an experience. If you travel for a long time over a long distance, you may get old in reality. That's why we cast rejuvenating magic on people so that they can come back young.

There is also a story about a man who returns home after 300 years and instantly ages when he opens the treasure box that he brought home. This story is actually related to space travel.

We cast rejuvenating magic, and we have various secrets on how to make people young again.

A Wow, the world where you live must be beautiful.

ETERNAL BEAUTY In that sense, we bring fashion, makeup, perfume, and other secrets necessary for becoming youthful to Earth. We are also involved in the entertainment industry.

They appear differently in the eyes of earthlings and non-earthlings

A On Earth, beautiful people are often associated with (the spirits of) foxes, like the nine-tailed fox, for example.

ETERNAL BEAUTY They are from the Pleiades.

A Oh, they are from the Pleiades. Are you different from them?

ETERNAL BEAUTY We are not Pleiadian.

A I see, so you are different.

ETERNAL BEAUTY We are not Pleiadian. I think it's difficult for you to see our true appearance. To you, our minds look like beautiful Eastern women wearing feather robes of heavenly maidens.

A Your minds appear...?

ETERNAL BEAUTY ...that way.

A You mean in the eyes of Pleiadians?

ETERNAL BEAUTY No, that's not what I mean. We are different from Pleiadians. I'm saying that we look that way to earthlings.

A When earthlings look at Pleiadians?

ETERNAL BEAUTY No. What I'm saying here has nothing to do with Pleiadians. When earthlings look at us, we look that way.

A What do you mean by "that way"?

ETERNAL BEAUTY Like I said, we look like beautiful Eastern women wearing feather robes of heavenly maidens.

A Oh, so you look like that to us.

ETERNAL BEAUTY Yes, that's right.

A What do you look like to someone who is not an earthling?

ETERNAL BEAUTY Well, it depends on who is looking. It's difficult to see what we truly are. Given that the Pleiades are the origin of nine-tailed foxes, you might have to think about what other species are related to beauty [*laughs*].

A You mean, there is a different type of beauty depending on the planet?

ETERNAL BEAUTY Yes. For example, in outer space, there are squirrel-like beings who can take the form of a human when necessary.

A I understand. You mean, they can sometimes take on a human form, right?

ETERNAL BEAUTY Yes, that's right. But it's difficult to find out their true form. In other words, they can shape-shift. We can, too. We have the ability to shape-shift, and we usually take on a form that is familiar to humans. Some space people appear as beautiful Scandinavian women, but we appear as Eastern women.

The origin of morals in Japanese women

ETERNAL BEAUTY I'm one of the people who cultivated the spirit of harmony of the Japanese people.
　We also often work to emphasize purity. For example, we express our pure love for our spouse, demonstrate our purity by sacrificing ourselves, or make our minds pure and transparent.

A   I see. Indeed, Princess Ototachibana was a self-sacrificing person.

ETERNAL BEAUTY   Yes. She showed self-sacrifice. This attitude has actually become the origin of morals in Japanese women.

A   Some people from other planets don't understand this trait.

ETERNAL BEAUTY   Yes, that's right.
   Also, the story of "being able to meet once a year" demonstrates the heart of endurance, which Japanese women possess. It is shown in their patience for their husband's return. Even in wartime, they continue to wait. When the husband is drafted as a soldier, the wife waits for his return patiently at home. This attitude has become the moral of wives.
   That's why, I, as a part of a cosmic soul, always watch over El Cantare and hope that His mission in this world will be fulfilled beautifully.

A   Oh, thank you very much for your support.

ETERNAL BEAUTY   We have continued to send Master the power of the "fountain of rejuvenation" so that he will stay pure and young eternally.

A Right. That's very important.

ETERNAL BEAUTY We still feel sorry that your movie *Daybreak* didn't end up as a beautiful work due to many problems, but we want to help you revive the story in some way so that it can remain eternally. We must preserve the story of "El Cantare in Youth" as an eternal legacy.

A Yes, what happened was quite a shame.

ETERNAL BEAUTY Yes, but it's merely a matter of this world. I believe time will resolve this problem.

A We may be able to re-film the movie.

ETERNAL BEAUTY I hope it'll be resolved in some other way. Please just pray. Please pray that something beautiful will come, or that something beautiful will manifest on earth and eternal beauty will come down to Happy Science.

A I understand. [Later in 2020, *Twiceborn* (Executive producer and original story by Ryuho Okawa) was released.]

Her views on the Shogun's "inner chambers"

A There are also men on your planet, right?

ETERNAL BEAUTY Yes, but the women usually stick together.

A Are there some men among the 50 people currently in your UFO?

ETERNAL BEAUTY Yes, there are some who have male functions, but there are mostly women here.

A I assume that your people are completely different from the female warriors, or the Amazons, but is your planet a kingdom that mainly consists of women?

ETERNAL BEAUTY Well, women tend to behave freely, so we have to protect their privacy in that regard.

A What do you think of Japanese *Ooku*, or the Shogun's inner chambers during the Edo period?

ETERNAL BEAUTY Hmm...Well...

A Is that part of Japanese culture, too?

ETERNAL BEAUTY Well, I think those kinds of chambers existed in all countries around the world and in all eras. Such chambers existed in all palaces, so I don't necessarily think that it's solely part of Japanese culture. I think it has a mixture of both heavenly and non-heavenly aspects.

A I understand.

About eternal love between a man and woman

A Do you have anything else you want to tell us?

ETERNAL BEAUTY I hope that Master Okawa will continue to be young and beautiful, and shine brilliantly for as many years as possible. I'm filled with such hopes.

A I definitely agree with you, but there are also enemy forces and...

ETERNAL BEAUTY You shouldn't recognize them as such. I hope He will continue to shine as a pure person despite living in this difficult world.

A Is there a way for us to maintain an environment that enables Him to remain that way?

ETERNAL BEAUTY I hope you'll use prayer more. There may be times when your mind is disturbed by worldly vibrations or when people look ugly to you, but please pray. We are always filled with such hopes. We are here with this mission. The eternally beautiful women are casting rejuvenating magic.

A Outer appearance is sometimes considered important. What do you think about external beauty on your planet? For example, some people may focus only on their outer appearance when they seek their partner. What do you think about that?

ETERNAL BEAUTY Our basic belief is that we should let our inner beauty manifest on the outside.

A So on your planet, does your inner beauty also manifest on the outside when you are born into a physical body?

ETERNAL BEAUTY Yes. We believe that those with inner beauty are also beautiful on the outside, and when they are born into a physical body, they are often born into a higher class. In this day and age, social classes have become rare, but I think everyone is looking for a way to make themselves shine brightly.

A Then, can we assume that space people with similar thoughts as yours live together on your planet?

Chapter Five

ETERNAL BEAUTY Yes, that's right.
I would be grateful if you could understand that there are people who are thinking about pure and eternal love and beauty all the time.

A Does your idea of eternal love ultimately lead to the idea of the "red string of fate" (a belief that destined lovers are connected to each other with an invisible red string)? Or is that a different idea?

ETERNAL BEAUTY Well, there are many different levels to eternal love. Some people will fall in love and unite on Earth, while others will fall in love with someone who has come from our planet and experience a once-in-a-lifetime romance. I think there are various cases. So, the love I'm talking about doesn't take place only on Earth. Sometimes, souls encounter those from other planets and fall in love.

A When we hear "eternal love," we understand it in the context of eternal love toward God. But when you say it in the context of a relationship between a man and woman, we who live on Earth are quick to assume that we are destined to love the same person throughout our lives.

ETERNAL BEAUTY As a matter of fact, it means that your love, or your acts of love, will remain eternally as something universal even after your physical body perishes. We are not saying that people will turn into zombies or Dracula to continue loving eternally. It's not like that.

A In romantic love, many ugly feelings and complications are often involved. For example, you and someone else could fall in love with the same person. When thinking about eternal love in this situation, how would you...

ETERNAL BEAUTY The true spirit remains only in *waka*, or Japanese poems. We believe that even though our physical bodies perish, our hearts and minds will remain forever.

I described my love in my poems, and they still remain even though more than a thousand years have passed.

A They continue to remain. I see.

ETERNAL BEAUTY Orihime is not the central planet in Vega, but is in the vicinity of Vega. And the stories that later became the folktales of Orihime and Hikoboshi, Princess Kaguya, and others were true stories that took place in the past over and over again. I would appreciate it if you could understand this to be true.

A I understand.
Lastly, when we pray, how should we address you?

Chapter Five

ETERNAL BEAUTY Well, it might sound like a grandiose name but please call me the "Goddess of the Milky Way," and your prayers will be heard.

A I see. I understand. Thank you very much.

RYUHO OKAWA OK.

UFO READING 21

CHAPTER SIX
A Space Battle in the Skies of Tokyo

Bazooka from Planet Zeta in the Magellanic Galaxies
Yaidron from Planet Elder

Recorded on December 3, 2018
at Happy Science Special Lecture Hall

Bazooka

A reptilian-type space being from Planet Zeta (also known as Planet Beta) in the Magellanic Galaxies. He loves war and interferes with disputes between countries and ethnic groups on Earth and continues to cause destruction. He is the enemy of Yaidron, who is a space being from Planet Elder in the Magellanic Galaxies and has the role of protecting El Cantare. Bazooka looks like a smaller version of Godzilla.

1

Bazooka's Simple Belief: Justice Lies with the Strong

A typical reptilian reappears

RYUHO OKAWA Is it showing on the camera?

A Yes, it is.

RYUHO OKAWA Is it?

A Please wait a moment, let me adjust the camera a bit...

RYUHO OKAWA The UFO is not so high up in the sky. It's not so far up.

A photo of a UFO that appeared in the Tokyo sky on December 3, 2018.

A I'm moving the camera. Let me zoom in and set it in place.

RYUHO OKAWA I don't think we'll be able to film for very long. It'll probably disappear quickly.

A I'm moving the camera slightly.

RYUHO OKAWA OK. We must be quick, otherwise, it may leave. Have you captured it?

A Yes. Please start. I've set the camera in place.

RYUHO OKAWA Who are you? Who are you?

A Oh, it's moving strangely... It's very unstable.

RYUHO OKAWA Yes, it's moving. Who are you?
 [*About 5 seconds of silence.*] The space person is saying, "You humans must realize how naive you are." We are being scolded. How troublesome.

A The UFO is moving around.

RYUHO OKAWA This could be difficult. He is scolding us about how naive humans are.

A Are you not human?

RYUHO OKAWA Are you not human?

A Are you a space person?

RYUHO OKAWA He says, "Of course."

A What planet is he from?

RYUHO OKAWA Which planet are you from? Please tell us.

SPACE PERSON Of course, I'm not human.

RYUHO OKAWA Then, what are you?

SPACE PERSON [*About 5 seconds of silence.*] I'm the enemy of Yaidron, the one who you have recently taken an interest in.

A [*Laughs wryly.*] Bazooka…

RYUHO OKAWA Are you Bazooka?

BAZOOKA Some people call me that.

A Oh, it's just you, Bazooka.

BAZOOKA You don't care about Bazooka?

A No, we don't. Because Bazooka is...

BAZOOKA What?

A ...nothing but an average, typical reptilian.

RYUHO OKAWA A typical reptilian...

A Yes, like "Godzilla."

RYUHO OKAWA [*To Questioner A.*] Is that why you sound so harsh?

A Yes.

RYUHO OKAWA Is he the "evil Godzilla"?

A Yes, he is.

RYUHO OKAWA An evil Godzilla.

A He has no faith and...

Chapter Six

RYUHO OKAWA He is a Godzilla without faith?

A A barbaric dinosaur who is behind the times.

RYUHO OKAWA Do you want to refute? Should a dinosaur be riding a UFO?
   Oh, it (the UFO) moved. It's moving a lot.

A All he says is that the strong will win.

BAZOOKA But that's the truth.

A And he just wants to magnify conflicts.

BAZOOKA That's not true. You have recently been watching *Seven Duels of Yagyu Jubei* (Japanese historical drama about a master swordsman) on TV, haven't you?

A OK. And?

BAZOOKA The strong always win. Our job is to completely destroy the ones who are trying to magnify conflicts.

A But last time, you said that you wanted to magnify conflicts.

BAZOOKA Well, that's... hmm...

A You didn't say anything about stopping conflicts.

RYUHO OKAWA Oh, the UFO might disappear.

A I think we still have time. It's still in the camera frame.

Anyway, we appreciate you moving your UFO randomly tonight; it makes it easier for us to spot you.

RYUHO OKAWA Right. It is moving around in a slightly unusual pattern.

A Yes. It's making typical UFO-like movements.

Bazooka's one-sided view of Master Okawa's dream about Former President George H.W. Bush

RYUHO OKAWA Isn't there more... Don't you have anything better to say? Are you trying to provoke us? Do you wish to fight us?

BAZOOKA Don't you want to know the truth behind Former President Bush's death?

A Master Okawa had a dream about the late Former President Bush about two weeks before he passed away.

Chapter Six

RYUHO OKAWA Yes, that's right.

A In Master's dream, there were 16 cows on a spaceship, along with Former President George H.W. Bush and his wife Barbara. And for some reason, Master Okawa was also there with them.

BAZOOKA So, you finally remember.

We showed him a specific scene when he got off the spaceship. He met Bush and Barbara, saw the 16 cows, and walked out onto a grass field from the open hatch of the spaceship. At that moment, he came back to his body and woke up.

A Does this dream have anything to do with your spaceship?

BAZOOKA We "kidnapped" him.

A What!?

BAZOOKA But just his soul.

A How dare you… What did you do to Master Okawa?

BAZOOKA We didn't do anything to his physical body.

A Then, what about Former President Bush?

BAZOOKA Bush's soul was already mostly out of his body.

A Is he on your side?

BAZOOKA The true nature of his soul is a reptilian, of course.

A Is he the same kind of reptilian as you?

BAZOOKA Yes.

A Oh, I see.

BAZOOKA He is our friend.

A I see.

BAZOOKA That's right.

Chapter Six

Questioning Bazooka's belief as a self-proclaimed swordsman

A Is it correct to assume that you are from Planet Zeta?

BAZOOKA You know, Zeta is...

A Oh! There's a small UFO blinking on the upper left of you.

BAZOOKA Yes. You know, we're looking for the opportunity to fight back.

A But you can't fight back, can you?

BAZOOKA If you think you can get rid of us like how the enemies in the Yagyu drama were defeated, you are mistaken. You won't have your way.

A Are you from Planet Zeta?

BAZOOKA You can call it that. Our planet can also be referred to in that way.

A All you care about is strength, don't you?

BAZOOKA I travel through space as a swordsman.

A But a swordsman needs the samurai spirit.

BAZOOKA I have it. A swordsman wins if he is strong. Justice lies with the strong.

A People call that plain murder.

BAZOOKA What are you saying?

A The TV drama (of Yagyu Jubei) said that a murderer and a swordsman are two different people.

BAZOOKA What? But the conclusion is the same.

A No, it's not!

BAZOOKA It's the same.

A It depends on whether there is spirituality behind their actions and whether their actions are taken from the perspective of justice...

BAZOOKA If you are weak, you'll lose, and that is when your mission will be over. In the end, justice won't be served.

A You don't understand Japanese Bushido, do you?

Chapter Six

BAZOOKA Our thoughts are incorporated in Bushido, too.

A No, it isn't.

BAZOOKA Yes, it is.

A Then, give me an example. Who were the reptilians that have appeared on Earth?

BAZOOKA Huh? Well...

A For example?

BAZOOKA It may be troublesome for you guys if I reveal their names.

A What do you mean?

BAZOOKA There might have been some in *Shinsengumi* (an elite group of swordsmen during the last days of the Edo period), you know? So, it may put you in a difficult situation.[1]

A Hmm... I'm not sure about that.

BAZOOKA Some people were moved to tears when they saw the members of Shinsengumi shedding tears (in a TV drama and a movie).

A But you can't cry for them, can you?

BAZOOKA Hey now. Don't you know the expression "crocodile tears" that is used on Earth?

A It means you aren't actually crying.

BAZOOKA Right. We cry "fake tears." Don't you know that the tears of reptilians are all fake?

Asking about Bazooka's superior

A But I'm sure Mr. Yaidron is different.

BAZOOKA That's why we're saying that we belong to different factions.

A Then, what kind of faction do you belong to?

BAZOOKA I belong to the faction of people who think, "All you need is strength."

A Who started that faction?

BAZOOKA What?

Chapter Six

A The founder.

BAZOOKA That's a difficult question. It's difficult to find out who the founder is.

A Is there no one above you?

BAZOOKA Well, we have a long history. It's too long to share with you. Our history is so long that it's almost as long as the history of the galaxies.

A Are you telling the truth?

BAZOOKA Yes.
　Hehehe... [*Laughs.*] People will interpret the founder's words in different ways in later years.

A But seeing as you don't understand self-sacrifice, love, the mind, or shedding tears, we feel that you are an inferior creature.

BAZOOKA That's not true. If you are truly strong, you can conquer others with a single strike or blow.

A But that would mean that you are very simple-minded.

BAZOOKA Say what you will. There is nothing you can do if there is a significant difference in strength between you and another. An ant can't win a battle against a dinosaur.

A That is why I'm saying that you are simple-minded.

BAZOOKA But there is no room for debate regarding a battle between a dinosaur and an ant.

A Do you even have debates on your planet?

BAZOOKA Basically, those in power represent justice, so all those who are inferior must succumb to that power.

A Then, do you admire people like Xi Jinping?

BAZOOKA Well, we are currently guiding him, so...

A Oh, I see.

BAZOOKA That goes without saying.

A Do you work under a supervisor?

BAZOOKA What?

Chapter Six

A Your boss.

BAZOOKA Why should I tell you such a secret?

A Well, you came all the way here tonight, so why don't you share some secrets with us?

BAZOOKA I came here because we're investigating what you are doing. I'm what you would call "PSIA (public security intelligence agency)."

A You'd have to be working under someone, then.

BAZOOKA There's no way I'd share such information with you.

A What's his name?

BAZOOKA Do you think the PSIA will tell you something like that? There's no way.

A But if you don't tell us...

Bazooka boasting about the dream prophecy

BAZOOKA I sent Ryuho Okawa a dream prophecy about the death of Former President Bush. We abducted him and the cows to teach him what an abduction is... That's why I invited him, Master of Happy Science, together with Mr. and Mrs. Bush and the cows.

A What is Master Okawa to you? Why did you feel it was necessary to go out of your way to tell Master Okawa about former President Bush's death?

BAZOOKA You've got it all wrong. He needs to understand how powerful we are.

Don't expect the U.S. to act as you wish for much longer; it won't continue. We are always lurking. So, don't think that China is your only enemy. You never know when the U.S. will fall under our control; its government changes every four years after all.

A What is your relation to President Trump?

BAZOOKA Hmm... Trump is similar to us, but he has a certain aim. He belongs to a different faction.

A Yaidron and his allies said that they are sending inspiration to Mr. Trump, as well.

Chapter Six

BAZOOKA Well, I guess you're right. They are currently trying to imbue him with certain tactics to add to his power.

A It's not tactics, it's spirit. They are trying to establish a spiritual foundation in what he is doing.

BAZOOKA I suppose you could call it spirit.

A One's actions are noble when there is spirit behind them.

BAZOOKA We don't like the idea that swordsmanship comes with enlightenment, or the oneness of swordsmanship and Zen.

A You probably don't even have the enlightenment of a swordsman or understand it.

BAZOOKA We don't need Zen.

A Why not?

BAZOOKA All we need to do is to kill.

A Then, you are no different from a machine.

BAZOOKA We eat our enemies anyway, so it doesn't matter.

A You mentioned Shinsengumi earlier, but did you delude them?

BAZOOKA Well, there were (souls of) reptilians among the members of Shinsengumi. It's an obvious fact.

A There were (souls of) reptilians on the opposing side, too, weren't there?

BAZOOKA Of course, there were.

A I suppose you reptilians can infiltrate any group.

BAZOOKA The people you like are all reptilians.

A No, that's not true.

BAZOOKA Manslayers are all reptilians. There's no doubt about it.
 We abducted 16 cows, took them to another planet, and transported them to a grass field. We also brought Former President Bush there. We showed all this to your Master and then showed him an Awa cattle (special beef cattle born and raised in Tokushima, Master Ryuho Okawa's birthplace) from among the 16 cows meeting a cruel death.

A Oh, so was that your declaration of war?

BAZOOKA In a way, we showed him his last moments.

A But I think humans are more evolved than you dinosaurs.

RYUHO OKAWA The upper one (UFO) disappeared.

A Then, that's goodbye.

RYUHO OKAWA OK.

2

Yaidron Works to Maintain Peace and Order in the Universe

The truth about Master Okawa's dream

RYUHO OKAWA Look. There are more UFOs. So many have come all at once. One, two, three, four, five, six... their numbers are increasing. There are so many of them today.

A Yes, there are. They all lit their ships because you came outside.

RYUHO OKAWA Wow... There are so many today.

A I'm going to stop recording temporarily.
[*Turns on the camera again and checks to see if the UFOs are in*

A photo of a UFO that appeared in the Tokyo sky on December 3, 2018.

the camera frame.] They look a little small. Please hold on for a moment.

RYUHO OKAWA But they look quite large to my eyes.

A Oh, here they are.

RYUHO OKAWA I hope you're not recording the smaller one below.

A I'm going to move the camera slightly. It's set in place now.

RYUHO OKAWA There is a small one down below.

A I'm moving the camera again.

RYUHO OKAWA OK. I think the big UFO is the one mainly observing us right now. It seems as though parts of it are invisible, but I can sense that it is quite the size... Oh, it moved just now. It's moving.

A Please hold on.

RYUHO OKAWA I wonder if it will come down. It looks like it wants to come down.

A Oh, no, no.

RYUHO OKAWA Can you capture the UFO in the camera frame?

A Oh, it's fine now.

RYUHO OKAWA Is it in the frame?

A Yes, it's good to go. Now, let's...

RYUHO OKAWA Can you see it?

A Yes, I can.

RYUHO OKAWA OK.
   Who are you? Who are you?

A I have set the camera in place.

RYUHO OKAWA Who are you? Who are you? You appear to be the central figure among the UFOs we are seeing today. He (the space person) is saying that he is Yaidron.

A Mr. Yaidron. Just as I thought.

Chapter Six

RYUHO OKAWA Yes. He says, "I'm Yaidron."

A Did you come because Bazooka was here?

YAIDRON We are keeping Bazooka in check.

A I thought so.

YAIDRON We won't let him do anything bad, so please don't worry.

A Thank you very much for your support, as usual.

YAIDRON We won't allow any evil actions to take place. Right now, Happy Science is trying to contain China and other forces based on the same strategy as us, so we won't let him get in your way. Please don't worry about that.

Bazooka said he abducted Master Okawa, but that's not true. When Master Okawa was asleep and his soul left his body for a short time, Bazooka came saying that he wanted to show him something. So, Master agreed and followed him on his own free will. That's all.

A I see...

YAIDRON It wasn't an abduction.

Asking about Bazooka's faction and its leader

RYUHO OKAWA Oh, the clouds have covered the UFO.

A Yes, the light of the UFO has become dim.

RYUHO OKAWA It's now covered by clouds.

A What faction does Bazooka belong to?

YAIDRON Well...

A Is he considered a typical reptilian?

YAIDRON I'd say it's a reckless faction. Or rather...

A Reptilians aren't the only ones in space who think that the strong always wins and that the winner is superior regardless of the situation, are they? There are many space people who think that way.

YAIDRON Yes. It's natural for people to think like that. But we believe a certain level of peace and order is necessary.

RYUHO OKAWA Another one appeared from below. There is one down there.

Chapter Six

A Is there anyone who is specifically in charge of guiding Bazooka?

YAIDRON The enemy's great in number, so it's difficult to pinpoint the person. Bazooka is the one who is always around this area, but I think there is definitely someone in charge of him.

A So, there is.

YAIDRON I think so. I'm sure the person above him is stationed in their mother ship.

A Is that person also a dinosaur-type?

YAIDRON I'm not sure if he is a dinosaur-type, but he surely has a mindset similar to dinosaur-type beings. Right now, I think they are giving China quite a powerful encouragement.

A Is that so?

YAIDRON Yes.

RYUHO OKAWA The light is shining brilliantly. The UFO is emitting intense light.

A Wow... But it's in the clouds.

RYUHO OKAWA I think it's below the clouds. Look at it, there.

A You're right.

RYUHO OKAWA The clouds are behind the UFO.

A I see that.

RYUHO OKAWA The clouds are higher, so the UFO is definitely under them.

Oh, I see a flying saucer. It's under the clouds. It's moving down. It's definitely under the clouds now.

A Can you see us, Mr. Yaidron?

YAIDRON Yes.

RYUHO OKAWA It's definitely not a star. The clouds are floating over it. The UFO is caught on the lower part of the clouds.

A Can we assume that the majority of people on Planet Elder think like you, Mr. Yaidron? Or are there also people who don't know which idea to support?

YAIDRON There are some people who were sent to Earth from Planet Elder and others who still remain on our planet. So there are slight differences in the way people think.

In any case, we are the ones who succeeded in defending our planet.

A Oh, I see. Those from Planet Zeta are the ones who failed to defend their planet, then.

YAIDRON Right.

Yaidron is on the lookout in the skies above Tokyo

A Uh-oh. It (the UFO) vanished.

RYUHO OKAWA The clouds may have covered it... They started producing clouds.

A Oh, but the UFO is still moving.

RYUHO OKAWA It's too bad they formed the clouds.

A I see. But the UFO can go through them. Oh, it's on camera again.

RYUHO OKAWA It came out. I think Yaidron is keeping Bazooka...

A Is he keeping Bazooka off?

RYUHO OKAWA Yes, that's right.
There are more UFOs below them, too. They've come out over there.

A Their protection is very much appreciated.

RYUHO OKAWA I think the UFOs down there are all part of Yaidron's alliance.
It's like a decisive battle of UFOs today. See, right above there... Oh, Bazooka already moved from here to there. Now, he's moving away even further...

A Oh, there are also three small UFOs in a row.

RYUHO OKAWA Right. There are more below and also on the sides. There are many of them.

A What shall we do? Should we end this talk now or should we investigate one more UFO?

RYUHO OKAWA Hmm... Mr. Yaidron, are there any other UFOs we should investigate?

YAIDRON I have brought five UFOs that are on my team. We are on high alert now.

A Oh, is that so? So the five of you are protecting us together.

YAIDRON Yes. We've taken up a position here in the sky, so you're safe.

A Wow, that's amazing. I didn't know there was such a battle taking place.

YAIDRON I heard Bazooka was here, so I brought five ships with me. There's no problem. We'll protect you at all costs.

A I wonder what it is that Bazooka wants to do.

RYUHO OKAWA What is Bazooka's aim? Is he plotting some kind of disorder or conflict?

It's true that there are opposition forces. They have their own agenda and are currently using the Belt and Road Initiative to cause chaos in various parts of the world. Perhaps a battle is inevitable, seeing as this is a battle over who takes control of Earth.

Bazooka's UFO seems larger than the rest—that one.

A By the way, what does your UFO look like today, Mr. Yaidron?

RYUHO OKAWA Oops, I think the large one is Mr. Yaidron's. Mr. Yaidron, please tell us what the ship you are on today looks like.

YAIDRON It's 70 meters (about 230 feet) in diameter.

A That's quite large.

YAIDRON Yes, it is. The diameter is 70 meters, and the height is about 15 meters (about 50 feet). It has the shape of a *dorayaki* (Japanese pancake sandwich with sweet red bean paste in the middle). Today, 35 people in total are on board.

A Do you do anything to relax?

YAIDRON Do you mean recreation?

A Are there any recreational activities you enjoy?

YAIDRON Well, we are always busy and on duty, so we don't have much time for recreation.

Chapter Six

The relationship between magic and willpower

A The other day, Hermes and Moses appeared in Master Okawa's dream. It was probably because Master Okawa is planning to give a lecture regarding magic very soon (the lecture "The Power to Make Miracles" was held on December 11, 2018 and is now compiled in *The Laws of Steel*). Is there some kind of relationship between magic and willpower?

YAIDRON Yes, there definitely is. Anyone can have willpower to a certain degree, though there may be a difference in strength. But unless you strengthen your willpower, you cannot use magic. To use magic, you must have control over a certain rule; this rule will be at work when you use magic.

What is more, magic is stronger than willpower; it's infectious. In other words, once your magical power reaches a certain level, you can grant it to someone else. Willpower belongs to the individual and you cannot transfer it to others. But magic can be used together by a group of people.

A I hear that Pleiadeans have magic and Vegans do, too.

YAIDRON Yes, they do. They all do.

A Are there different ways of casting magical energy depending on the planet?

YAIDRON It all has to do with how they express their spiritual self in the third dimension. They are all trying to express themselves in this three-dimensional world by using magic.

Without magic, you tend to forget that you are a spiritual being. In other words, using magic requires you to concentrate your mind and to know about the invisible forces that are at work. So, although you have a physical body, you need to understand that your physical body is not your true self and that the mind lies deep inside of you.

Of course, fighting requires willpower. But willpower cannot be more than what it is. Magic is different. For example, even a politician can start using magic when he or she becomes very popular. Using magic also means attracting and absorbing the willpower of other people and exerting it as a collective power. It is similar to the way the power of faith works.

How to develop the ability to use psychic binding and electric shock

A On Planet Elder, can everyone who was born there use magic?

YAIDRON No, they must go through training.

Chapter Six

A So, training is required?

YAIDRON Training is necessary, and the power of the group also matters.

A The power of the group?

YAIDRON When people gather as a team, they can exert a stronger power. There are textbooks or guidebooks on magic to teach them according to their level.

A This may not be exactly what you are talking about, but do you have schools that teach magic, much like Hogwarts in *Harry Potter*?

YAIDRON It is not quite the same but there are some... We have the ability to bestow our power to those who need it. It is a power that is not just physical strength... Well, we also train our bodies, but as you train your body, your mind also gets stronger, doesn't it?

A Yes.

YAIDRON When your mind becomes stronger, your willpower also becomes stronger. And when your willpower becomes stronger, a spiritual field begins to form. For example, when you feel a strong murderous intent directed at you, you become unable to move. It is sort of like that. In your movie, *The Laws of the Universe—Part 1*, there is a scene where the enemy is tied up by willpower or something like a golden rope, right?

A Yes.

YAIDRON People become capable of restraining others with their willpower as depicted in the movie.

A I see. It is like a binding seal.

YAIDRON Yes. They acquire the power to do such things.

A Then, what about the electric shock? How can one do it?

YAIDRON Well, to do that... You need to draw power from space people like us.

A I see. So, we must draw power from outer space.

YAIDRON Yes, that's right. It's very easy. In your case, your voice reaches us, so if you have some kind of trouble...

A We just have to call out your name and say, "Mr. Yaidron!" right?

Chapter Six

YAIDRON Ask me for support by saying, "Yaidron, release the electric shock!" before you face the enemy, and say, "Electric shock! Crush the enemy!" Then, our powers will flow through you.

A Cool! Where does your planet's electric shock come from?

YAIDRON Well, if I go into detail, it will take a while to explain.

A Oh, I see.

YAIDRON The source of our power connects all the way to God—the Origin, so we would have to explain what God is.

A I understand.

YAIDRON It's not so simple.

What Yaidron thinks about to maintain safety in the universe

A Does the type of magic differ depending on the planet?

YAIDRON Yes, it does. Some use magic just to be beautiful, while others use the beauty that they've obtained to lure people with their sex appeal or foxiness to achieve their goals. There are those who are content as long as they appear beautiful and others who want to gain money, social standing, prestige, or other things with that beauty. There are people like that.

We, on the other hand, don't use the kind of magic that the nine-tailed foxes (bewitching spirit, or a kind of *yokai* monster) use. Our magic is more like the "Force." We are currently trying our best to use the "Force of justice."

A I see. I understand.

YAIDRON We, too, have the power to kill various beings, but we constantly ask ourselves whether there is justice in our actions or whether our actions are considered right. We always think about whether our intentions and the outcomes are right.

We are keeping watch over the universe with the intent of maintaining peace and order. We never do anything cruel.

A I see... Then, you mean that there are people in outer space who are protecting the security and order of the universe, much like there are forces that work to protect the security and order on Earth?

YAIDRON Yes, that's right. Whenever Bazooka comes, like he did today, I'm also here on guard with five ships. It's important to keep the enemy in check; we are no different from Japan's Self-Defense Forces.

A Is it possible for your ship to communicate with Bazooka's ship? Can UFOs do that?

YAIDRON Well, we can communicate through telepathy, so…

A Oh, so communication is done through telepathy?

YAIDRON Yes. As long as we are here, they cannot do anything. We are always watching them, especially these past few days.

A What will you do if something stronger than Bazooka arrives?

YAIDRON If something stronger comes, we will call for backup. We still have many other allies. If I think we need more power, I'll gather them. We have many other allies in the Interplanetary Alliance.

A So you have many allies.

YAIDRON We can call for their support. If we do, more than 100 ships will surely arrive. If we have to show you our UFO fleet, we can do that.

Today, there are just 10 ships on our side in total. They are around us now.

A I see. Thank you very much.

YAIDRON I'm quite strong myself, so it won't be easy for them to fight against me. As long as I'm here, it won't be easy for them to win, so there'll be no problem.

A We appreciate your support.

YAIDRON We'll protect you, so don't you worry.

A OK.

Romance on Planet Elder

YAIDRON Is something bothering you?

A Hmm...

YAIDRON Anything in particular?

A Well, let me see...

Chapter Six

YAIDRON I guess the big event is coming up, isn't it? The celebration...

A Yes. The El Cantare Celebration (Master's lecture) is...

YAIDRON The event is in about a week, so there may be some space people who are plotting to disturb Master.

A Do people on Planet Elder also have romance?

YAIDRON [*Laughs.*] That's quite the curveball.

A [*Laughs.*] The other day, you said that you technically have a marriage system.

YAIDRON Well... hmm... [*Laughs.*] It's embarrassing to answer such a question.

A OK [*laughs*].

YAIDRON Well, how should I put it? Women tend to admire strong people, don't they?

A I see, yes.

YAIDRON That's something that happens on our planet, too. The women on our planet admire the strong and feel that they want to have children with them. They have feelings like that.

A By strength, do you mean the kind of strength you mentioned earlier?

YAIDRON Unless you are truly strong, you cannot be kind.

A I see! That's what the Japanese actor Junichi Okada said.

YAIDRON A truly strong man is kind. Women are drawn to men who are strong and kind.

A I see. That's the same with earthlings.

YAIDRON Depending on the time period, we take various measures and sometimes put our lives on the line to protect Earth. We always stand on the side of the heroes.

A I see. I understand.

YAIDRON Everything will be alright. We are stationed right above you.

A I can see something that has a really interesting shape.

RYUHO OKAWA Where?

A I'm going to stop filming for a moment. Thank you very much for your time, Mr. Yaidron.

YAIDRON Sure.

The battle formation of the UFOs to stand against Bazooka

RYUHO OKAWA I think those three ships are a line of defense against Bazooka.

A I wish they'd show up on the camera screen.

RYUHO OKAWA They may be too small to capture. They might be doing something against Bazooka...

A Bazooka's ship is showing up on the screen.

RYUHO OKAWA This... This formation is unnatural.

A Yes, it's quite unnatural.

RYUHO OKAWA It's odd. Maybe they are doing something to...

A Oh, is it this one? The three ships are showing up on the screen now.

RYUHO OKAWA They are lined up to face Bazooka. It's clearly a formation to launch an attack.

A Wow—how amazing.

RYUHO OKAWA This must be their line of defense.
 [*About 5 seconds of silence.*] They are lined up vertically. It's quite unusual.
 [*About 5 seconds of silence.*] Above them, there seem to be a few more. They are forming a line of defense.

A They must be defending us.

RYUHO OKAWA No matter how we look at it, it is a line of defense against Bazooka.
 [*About 5 seconds of silence.*] There are one, two, three, four, five, six, seven, eight, and nine—about nine ships.

A Oh, there are some underneath... Only two are showing up on the screen, but there are actually three.

RYUHO OKAWA There are 10 ships, not including Bazooka's.

Chapter Six

A Wow.

RYUHO OKAWA It is just as Mr. Yaidron said.

A He stationed them there.

RYUHO OKAWA Yes. They are on high alert.

A I wanted to record the three ships that are in a row but...

RYUHO OKAWA They aren't showing on the screen, are they?

A I think only some of them in the middle have shown up.

RYUHO OKAWA Hmm... Not all three?

A Unfortunately, no.

RYUHO OKAWA Hmm...

A I'm moving the camera a bit.

RYUHO OKAWA It's true that Mr. Yaidron has come to defend...

A Yes, he has.

RYUHO OKAWA He said that 10 ships were here. These must be the ones he was talking about.

A Yes. It's amazing.

RYUHO OKAWA They have formed a defensive arc with some ships, plus three lined up vertically in the front and two in the back. Yaidron is in the very back.

A I'm moving the camera again. It's a shame I cannot film the three UFOs in a row.

RYUHO OKAWA Yes, it is. We can see them with our eyes, though.

A Yes. Only the largest one shows up on the screen.

RYUHO OKAWA Yes.

A I think it's best that we end here.

RYUHO OKAWA Are you sure?

A Yes. Thank you very much.

Chapter Six

RYUHO OKAWA We've confirmed that they have come.

[*About 5 seconds of silence.*] They are not so high up. They are at an altitude of about 300 to 500 meters (about 980-1640 feet). It's amazing—absolutely amazing.

A It is as if a space war is taking place in the sky...

RYUHO OKAWA They are fighting a space war. It's amazing. It's just like *Star Wars*.

A We actually saw the UFOs lighting up all at once.

RYUHO OKAWA Right. They suddenly lit up one after another. They were about to form a fleet.

A I think so, too.

RYUHO OKAWA When dozens of UFOs get together, they form a fleet—a UFO fleet.

A Thank you very much.

TRANSLATOR'S NOTE

1 According to spiritual readings conducted by Happy Science, some staff members were born as members of Shinsengumi in their past lives.

UFO READING 23

CHAPTER SEVEN

Battle of Values in the Universe

Bazooka from Planet Zeta in the Magellanic Galaxies

Yaidron from Planet Elder

Mycenae from Planet Honeykaney in Scorpius

Recorded on December 15, 2018
at Happy Science Special Lecture Hall in Japan

1

Bazooka—The One Who Calls Himself the "Creator of Fear"

A UFO boldly positioned in front of the Moon

A I'll start filming.

RYUHO OKAWA Is it appearing on camera?

A Yes. Let me zoom in slightly. It appears to be next to the Moon.

RYUHO OKAWA Yes. It is intentionally stationed in the direction of the Moon for us to see. Is it in the camera frame?

A I'm still moving the camera. I'm zooming in now.

A photo of a UFO (bottom right) that appeared near the Moon (upper left) in the Tokyo sky on December 15, 2018.

Chapter Seven

RYUHO OKAWA How does it look?

A It's in the frame.

RYUHO OKAWA OK. There is a UFO that is boldly stationed right in front of the Moon. I have a hunch that it's one we haven't seen before.

It may move. I'm not sure whether it will go up or down, but if it goes down, it will be hidden behind the trees, and we'll lose sight of it.

The UFO is shining in the moonlight. We can see it in the direction of the Moon, and I think it's relatively close to where we are. It is staying there. We usually don't see something like this. It has boldly positioned itself in the moonlight. To the naked eye, it looks orange in color. I think it's very close to us. The UFO is not so high in altitude and we're only about 300 to 500 meters (985-1640 feet) away from it. It's not that far. I think we are less than 1 km (half a mile) away from each other.

Let me see... It's to the west of us, I think.

A Oh, it moved a bit lower.

RYUHO OKAWA Is it coming down?

A Yes, a little...

RYUHO OKAWA It's going to disappear or hide soon. We'd better hurry, or it'll hide behind the trees.

A OK. Then, where is it from?

RYUHO OKAWA OK. Where are you from? Please tell us.

The one who has appeared near the Moon—where did you come from? Please tell us.

[*About 5 seconds of silence.*] The space person is saying, "Too bad for you, I'm not Yaidron. It's me, Bazooka" [*laughs wryly*].

A [*Laughs wryly.*] Oh, it's Bazooka.

RYUHO OKAWA That's disappointing. He's here by himself.

A Maybe that's why the mic broke earlier.

RYUHO OKAWA The space person is saying he is Bazooka. It has been a while since he last came to us.

Bazooka's idea of justice and what he believes to be the principles of the universe

A What do you want?

BAZOOKA Hey, don't be so hateful.

A What? Do you even like us?

BAZOOKA There's a chance that I'm the one on the side of justice, you know.

A What is your idea of justice?

BAZOOKA My idea of justice means to help the strong and crush the weak.

A So you'll crush the weak.

BAZOOKA Yes. It's important to weed out the weak. I believe the principles of the universe lie in weeding out the weak.

A Which group are you the captain of?

BAZOOKA I don't understand what you mean by that. If you are the enemy, then we're the first line of attack.

A So you are in the first squad.

BAZOOKA Yes, of course.

A How many superiors do you have?

BAZOOKA We don't have what you call "superiors." We operate as a group, but right now, I'm acting alone, as you can see. My ship is the only one that's keeping a lookout.

A How many people can ride your ship?

BAZOOKA Five people.

A The capacity is smaller than I expected.

BAZOOKA This UFO isn't for combat; it's for monitoring.

A Were you the one who had a Godzilla or dinosaur-like appearance?

BAZOOKA That's not a very flattering way of describing me.

A Are there five beings who look like that riding your ship?

BAZOOKA There are five beings that don't look human.

Chapter Seven

A I see. But there must be a person who is giving you orders.

BAZOOKA We have a mother ship. For a five-person UFO to visit Earth, there needs to be a mother ship above.

A In that case, is the leader on that mother ship?

BAZOOKA The fact that the leader hasn't come out means he must be cautious.

A Why do you come to Happy Science and to where Master Okawa is so often?

BAZOOKA He is too kind.

A Too kind? To whom?

BAZOOKA To living beings.

A But you are also a living being.

BAZOOKA Well, I...

A Oh wait, the light is about to disappear.

RYUHO OKAWA Yes, the ship may disappear from the frame soon.

BAZOOKA Our mother ship is hiding in the moonlight so that it can't be spotted. It's in the direction of the Moon. It is actually hiding.

A I'm going to move the camera slightly.

RYUHO OKAWA It will be out of frame soon.

BAZOOKA I'll be going soon so ask your questions quickly.

A You are also a living creature, right? Oh, it's in the frame again.

BAZOOKA Well, based on the definition of a living creature, yes, I am. But I actually transcend living beings.

A What do you mean by that?

BAZOOKA I am a killing machine or the creator of fear.

A Do you want to instill fear in people?

BAZOOKA Uh-huh.

A So you enjoy seeing human beings in fear?

Chapter Seven

BAZOOKA I'm more interested in the relationship between the controller and the controlled. This is one of the principles in the universe. This relationship, or a hierarchy between the rulers and the ruled, is one of the principles that govern the universe. I'm the one who represents this principle.

A I see. Then, do you think that a society based on a class system is better?

BAZOOKA If there's no clear difference between the strong and the weak, or between the righteous and the wrong, the order in the universe cannot be maintained. The ones who firmly believe in this idea are on my side of the group.

A So that's why you prefer the style of rule practiced in communist regimes like in China, where only a small number of elites and top executives of the communist party have absolute power, while the rest of the people are told to be equal.

BAZOOKA You may think it's evil because it's about another country and not yours. But suppose someone among your friends starts to disagree or rebel against you. You'd become upset, wouldn't you? For example, if your friend bad-mouths you, I'm sure you'd be upset. What I'm saying is that the outcome is the same: people will be divided into the rulers and the ruled.

Bazooka thinks getting quick results is more important than having love or mercy

A Then, your way of thinking...

BAZOOKA We are just too smart.

A No, it doesn't mean you are smart. Rather, it means you have a simplistic way of thinking.

BAZOOKA We are quick to come to a conclusion.

A But you are so simple...

BAZOOKA We are quick to judge.

A I think it means you don't understand love or mercy.

BAZOOKA We are quick to come to a conclusion. We just destroy the enemy. We make a quick decision and take the easy approach. We completely destroy the obstacle at hand. This makes things so much easier in most cases. The larger the country, the more they need to take this kind of approach. Unlike in a small country, it's difficult to reach a consensus in a large country, so things need to be dealt with using force.

Even Japan does the same thing sometimes. For example, the people of Okinawa expressed their opposition against the reclamation work in Henoko (for the relocation of the U.S. military base) through the gubernatorial election, but the Japanese government pushed through with their decision and had the Ministry of Defense continue with the reclamation work. There are times when you have to force your way through.

A In such instances, you simply carry it out by force, don't you?

BAZOOKA Yes, absolutely. If you talk about love or protecting the weak in a case like that, nothing will proceed.

So you cannot completely dismiss our principles. Even Yaidron cannot. He and his allies have a different way of thinking and they sometimes use a soft approach, but if you look at the outcome, what we are doing is the same—they are a little dumber than us, that's all.

A [*Laughs wryly.*] Are they?

BAZOOKA The conclusion is the same, anyway.

A But I don't think having love or mercy makes you stupid.

BAZOOKA Love and mercy are just camouflages to hide the fact that you are a devil.

A I don't think they are camouflages.

BAZOOKA Without them, people won't be able to tell whether you are a devil or not. Even God shows anger and punishes people at times, right? Yaidron also says he shows his anger and punishes people. Those are his true colors, but he simply pretends to have love and mercy to make himself look like an angel.

A But there is a Being who created creatures like you in the first place.

BAZOOKA Yes, there's a smart one.

A It's not about smartness. The Being accepts you as you are and allows you to exist in the universe.

BAZOOKA We could trample over ant-like creatures like you at any time. But there is a Being who chooses to watch you patiently over a long period of time. That's why we try to find the balance between our opinions and yours.

Yaidron also causes floods, earthquakes, and tsunamis occasionally, you know.

Chapter Seven

A Oh, I know why you are saying those things. Yaidron has become famous at Happy Science, so you wish to make your name known as well, don't you?

BAZOOKA Of course, I do. I'm his rival, so I have to contend.

RYUHO OKAWA Your UFO is the only one here from your side. You must be feeling lonely.

A Right. It must be lonely to be the only UFO here with five people aboard.

BAZOOKA We have no chance of winning now; I just came to keep an eye on you.

A Is your group and mother ship planning to control China?

BAZOOKA We're in hiding at the moment.

A Where are you from? Oh, I remember. You're from Planet Zeta of the Magellanic Galaxies.

BAZOOKA That's right.

A Why did you lose the battle on Planet Zeta?

BAZOOKA Well, I guess we fell into a trap because we tend to rush to get quick results. They laid out a trap because they knew that our wit would make us jump on the bait.

A I see. That's how you see it.

BAZOOKA A species like ours is necessary for the evolution of humanity. Without our way of thinking, there wouldn't be surgical operations. Surgical operations are quite brutal, don't you think? Usually, you wouldn't think you can cure an illness by cutting out the diseased part of the body. But illnesses cannot be cured by traditional Eastern medicine.

A But when surgeons operate, they do so with the wish that the patient will get better. Does that mean you also have this kind of feeling?

BAZOOKA Well, I can't say that I have much of it. Removing the bad parts would be the priority.

A But don't you take out the bad parts hoping that the person will get better?

BAZOOKA It's not my role to have such hopes.

A If you had such hopes, it would mean that you have love within you.

BAZOOKA That's the way religious leaders think; "surgeons" like us only focus on removing the bad parts.

A So you simply think of it in the mechanical sense?

BAZOOKA It's a logical way of thinking. It doesn't matter if a doctor is an atheist or anything else. As long as the results are good, there's nothing wrong with it. We don't think about it so deeply. We just focus on the results without having any particular emotion.

An invader's opinion on *The Laws of the Universe—Part 1*

A In our movie, *The Laws of the Universe—Part 1*, the reptilian character named Zamza ultimately awakens to faith and becomes a faith-minded reptilian. What did you think of Zamza after watching the movie?

BAZOOKA Pitiful. She should be eaten.

A So that's how you think.

BAZOOKA Yeah.

A What about Dahar (an evil alien character in the movie that came from the flip-side universe)? Would you want to follow his leadership?

BAZOOKA Dahar is cool. I'd give him more weapons.

A But Dahar is only mad because he was confined to the flip-side universe. He is on the losing side and is acting like a sore loser.

BAZOOKA Well, that was... No, no, no, he just needed to call for more support.

A Seeing him, did you think he was cool?

BAZOOKA I did. His army was so large—overwhelmingly so.

A But he lost in the end.

BAZOOKA No. He only looks defeated because you were the ones depicting him based on your perspective. From their perspective, they managed to invade Earth. He attacked his enemy's main base, didn't he? So...

A It seems you and I need to have a long talk.

Chapter Seven

BAZOOKA Alpha (the God of Earth), or "The Beginning," was almost defeated at the end of the movie. Gaia (the goddess who is the wife and protector of Alpha) virtually lost. The invaders broke through her spiritual powers toward the end, so she was almost beaten. It was a narrow escape.

A But Lord Alpha won in the end.

BAZOOKA Alpha would have died if he were older.

A Do you have a certain lifespan?

BAZOOKA We do, but at the same time, we don't. I'm not sure how to phrase it, but we get reused multiple times. If we malfunction, we are repaired.

A Do you have parents?

BAZOOKA Huh? What do you mean?

A Do people on your planet have parent-child relationships?

BAZOOKA We don't think like that. A certain number of eggs are laid and once they hatch, they go through training. As they are trained, they are ranked, and the strongest ones are raised as elites. That's how we think.

A You are like cyborgs.

BAZOOKA You may say so, but from God's perspective, everyone is a cyborg.

A That's not true.

BAZOOKA It is.

A Well, let's end the talk here.

BAZOOKA Fine, OK.

A Thank you very much.

RYUHO OKAWA His UFO will go off-screen soon.

A Right. Thank you very much for today.

RYUHO OKAWA Then, let's examine the other UFO over there... It seems like we have a lot of allies today.

2

Yaidron's Power to Protect the Savior

The reason for Bazooka's visit

RYUHO OKAWA At an altitude of about 400 meters (about 1300 feet), there is an object that is lighting up.

[*About 10 seconds of silence.*] Can you record it?

A Please wait a moment.

[*About 10 seconds of silence.*] Yes, I have it on camera.

RYUHO OKAWA Is it in frame?

A Yes.

RYUHO OKAWA Is it?

A I managed to get it in the frame this time.

RYUHO OKAWA OK.

A The camera is ready.

RYUHO OKAWA There are no clouds today, so the UFO looks no different from a star. At first glance, it looks like a star, but in my eyes, there is a light shining at about 400 meters above ground. It is right above us, and I think it is stationed in a place where it can get a good view of the whole area. I think this is the main UFO...

There is something moving over there. Oh, never mind. It's just a helicopter. Either a helicopter or a jet is flying by. That's not the one we are talking about.

Then, let's ask them. The one on camera, who are you? Please tell us. Are you Yaidron?

[*About 5 seconds of silence.*]

YAIDRON Of course, this is Yaidron.

A Did you come because Bazooka was around?

A photo of a UFO that appeared in the Tokyo sky on December 15, 2018.

YAIDRON We're in position here with a dozen ships. So he is no threat to us. He has come with only one ship, so he doesn't stand a chance. Please don't worry.

Bazooka is up to no good.

A Is he?

YAIDRON Yes, he is plotting something. Right now, he is targeting Master Okawa's eldest son. Bazooka is scheming to sneak into him to somehow create an opportunity to attack Master.

A This may be rude, but doesn't he have anything better to do?

YAIDRON The presence of Master Okawa is essential in establishing correct values on Earth, which will lead to establishing correct values in the universe. I heard that the chairperson of Happy Science is insisting on publishing the spiritual message from Mao Zedong as soon as possible. The enemy is responding to this, in fear that their intervention might be exposed. The book will reveal the relationship between China, Bazooka, and the flip-side universe.

But you successfully held the El Cantare Celebration, to which many people came, and you've shown that Happy Science won't waver at all. That's why he (Master's eldest son) is desperately trying to disturb you. I think your believers understand the situation. Everyone is starting to understand why he became the way he is now. The reasons behind it are gradually being revealed.

So there's nothing to worry about. What is occurring in Japan now is a revolution on a global scale. That's why every move Happy Science makes is very important. The mass media should be reporting your activities. It's wrong of them to interfere or be critical of your activities and only report on the one who has dropped out. Don't worry about that.

Yaidron's defense power and his physical development

YAIDRON Is there something you wish to ask me?

A Today...
You are becoming famous in Happy Science.

YAIDRON Yes. I sense that people (of Happy Science) are thinking of me as the protector (of Master Okawa).

A I think everyone is praying (to you for Master Okawa).

Chapter Seven

YAIDRON I know. We are protecting the Lord from above. Even if a missile were to be fired, for example, we would shoot it down. Our defensive capability is higher than the Self-Defense Forces. You will all be dead if a Self-Defense Forces officer in charge sleeps through an incoming missile, but we won't make that mistake. We have a system that alerts us of imminent danger.

What if North Korea or China were to shoot a missile or send ninja squads from above? You can't rule out the possibility.

A No, we can't.

YAIDRON It won't always be a spirit that comes to attack you; it could be a real-life person. In both cases, we can fight to protect you. That's what we have been doing.

A By the way, does everyone on Planet Elder have horns?

YAIDRON Yes, but there are differences among people because they have different personalities. Aggressive people tend to have horns that point to the front, while less aggressive people tend to have horns that curve back, like a goat. In the latter case, their horns show that they have no intention to fight.

A There is another light coming into the frame from the bottom.

RYUHO OKAWA Yes, it seems so. Are you talking about the one that looks like a star below Yaidron's ship?

A In the camera frame, it looks quite large.

RYUHO OKAWA Is that so? Is it that one?

A I think so...

RYUHO OKAWA We usually can't capture this many UFOs...

A They are all moving.

RYUHO OKAWA Oh, I see. There is another one right below the one that you just found.

A Yes. Mr. Yaidron, do those ships belong to your comrades?

YAIDRON They're our convoy fighters.

A So, is everyone born with horns?

YAIDRON No, that's not the case [*laughs*]. The horns gradually grow.

A Oh, I see. Interesting. You are like a deer.

YAIDRON The horns grow with age and according to the individual's roles and needs. They also break off and grow again, if necessary.

I'm not sure if we can say that our bodies age, but we actually shed our skin according to our development. We can shed our old skin for our new body to emerge. Our skin cracks open so that we can shed the old layer for the new body to come out.

A I see. Wow.

Yaidron's face, weapon, outfit, and skin color

A What does your face look like?

YAIDRON Oh, my face. Well...

A Are you hesitant to share?

YAIDRON No, not really. I don't mind sharing it. I'd have to say that my face is most similar to Superman's.

A Oh, is that so!?

YAIDRON Yes. I look like him. I'm quite handsome.

A I'd imagine so.

YAIDRON I'm fairly handsome.

A I had a feeling that you might be [*laughs*].

YAIDRON If I grow my hair out, I might be able to hide my horns. I could probably hide them if I have a punk look.

A I see.

I'm going to move the camera a bit. The UFO is moving upward.

So you take on a human form.

YAIDRON Yes, I look that way. I don't look like a Japanese ogre, who only wears tiger-skin shorts [*laughs*].

A So you are not an ogre that looks like "Kaminari-san" (a thunder god).

YAIDRON Well, I can take that form, too, if I want to. If I'm meeting people from the past, I may take that form. All I have to do is wield an iron club, right?

I don't actually have an iron club, but I do have other weapons. It's not a staff of Kerykeion (caduceus) though...

A The other day, you said you have an electric whip.

Chapter Seven

YAIDRON [*Laughs.*] Yes, I have that, too.

A Oh, does that mean you have several weapons, then?

YAIDRON I have several types of weapons attached to my belt.

A I know Wonder Woman (in the movie) also has a whip.

YAIDRON I have a short 15-centimeter (6-inch) baton on my waist. When I press the button on it, it can become an electric whip, a sharp tool, or a stick that can stretch like a *nyoi-bo* (a magical stick that shrinks and extends at will). But that's not the only weapon I have; I have about four different types of weapons.

A Is it alright for you to reveal this? Given that there are still a lot of enemies, should I refrain from asking about your weapons?

YAIDRON These tools are only used during close combat or hand-to-hand combat. I usually use supernatural powers instead, so I don't use these weapons often. They're only there in case I have to fight physically.

A What kind of clothes do you wear?

YAIDRON When you say clothes...

A Space suit.

YAIDRON Well, I wear an elastic outfit.

A What color is it?

YAIDRON I can change my outfit. I own several kinds to fit my mood. Right now, I'm wearing a moss-green color.

A Is your skin color also like Superman's?

YAIDRON Well, if I take off my clothes... Are you curious? You might be able to see it when I take a bath for just 30 seconds. During those 30 seconds, you can see me naked.

A What do you look like?

YAIDRON [*Laughs.*] Well, how do I put it? Hmm... I think I look Caucasian.

A I see.

Chapter Seven

About Yaidron's superpowers and his psychic binding

A Do you look at yourself in a mirror every day?

YAIDRON [*Laughs.*] Well, I can if I want to.

A Do you not use a mirror so often?

YAIDRON Well, how should I explain it? Unlike you, we can look at ourselves from the outside.

A Oh, so you don't need to use things like mirrors.

YAIDRON No. We can see ourselves from the outside. You may need mirrors to do so, but we don't. We can look at our appearance from the outside if we want to.

A Is that a type of supernatural power?

YAIDRON It is. We can split off part of our soul that embodies the functions of our eyes to see ourselves.

A I see. Does that power become like the power of remote viewing that Master Okawa uses when it is developed to an exceptional level?

YAIDRON That's right. We can do that, too. We can get a 360-degree view of ourselves in the way others see us.

A Do you have a father and a mother?

YAIDRON Oh, yes. I have both a father and a mother.

A Are they on Planet Elder?

YAIDRON Yes. My father was also a great commander.

A Oh, is that so?

YAIDRON Yes. So it runs in our blood.

A Wow.
   I heard that you had warded off some spirits the other day.

YAIDRON Warded off?

A Yes, you created a spiritual screen during the El Cantare Celebration.

YAIDRON Oh, yes I did.

A How did you do that? Is there a trick to it?

YAIDRON We can radiate rays of light from above. I'm not sure how to explain it, but the light spreads from a central point like a skirt, or a yurt, to create a barrier that wards off or prevents *ikiryo* (spirits of living people) and evil spirits from coming close.

A I see. You mean, a spiritual screen around Master Okawa, right?

YAIDRON Yes. We can protect him in this way.

A Wow. That's amazing.

YAIDRON We can protect him like this, and that's what we've been doing.

Now is an extremely important time. We need him to go as far as to unveil the truth about our world, so we must protect him at any cost.

Yaidron's relationship with Metatron

A Before we finish, let me ask about one more topic. We just watched a movie titled *Angels & Demons*. I was curious to know your thoughts on this movie.

YAIDRON There are many conflicts on earth. If you consider all conflicts as evil, you won't be able to distinguish the angels from the devils. When there is a conflict, it is usually a battle for justice, or a battle to see where God's Will lies. In the case of battles between different ethnic groups, it's hard to see which side justice lies on. The answer may not be clear for a long period of time. It could take a thousand or even three thousand years to know which side was right. When there is a big event like the sinking of a continent, you can't always tell if it was the work of angels or devils. Depending on the level of your awareness, things will appear differently.

RYUHO OKAWA The UFO has gone much higher up today than it did yesterday. It is high up.

A Yes, but it's still in the frame.

RYUHO OKAWA Oh, that's good.

A I think many angels' names come from Judaism. Did the ethnic groups living in Israel originally come from different planets?

YAIDRON Well, during the rise of a civilization, many space people tend to gather, so you can't necessarily say that there is only one species of space people immigrating there. When they are born Jewish, they'll live as a Jew, but they all have different opinions and do various things.

I call myself Yaidron, and one of my well-known friends calls himself Metatron.

A Is Metatron a seraph?

YAIDRON Yes. He was well-known in the past. He is actually my friend.

A I see.

YAIDRON Yes. His name has remained much longer in history than mine has.

A Metatron and Sandalphon and...

YAIDRON Yes. They, too, intervened in Earth's affairs. Judaism also has a punishing god, so it is indeed difficult to distinguish gods from devils. However, whether they are God's messengers or not makes a big difference.

A I'm surprised. You are so knowledgeable.

YAIDRON Yes. [*Using Ryuho Okawa's body to point to the sky.*] There, look at that small ship. That's a small convoy fighter.

A Yes. I thought I saw another light shining in the middle of the frame.

YAIDRON Yes. It's close, but you probably can't see it yet.

A I'm not sure.

YAIDRON You can take a picture...

A There seems to be one more ship that is sending us very strong thoughts. Is it from a different planet?

YAIDRON You should talk to the red one over there.

A Oh, the red one. I see. Then, we'll see you again.

YAIDRON OK.

A Thank you very much.

Chapter Seven

3

Mycenae from Planet Honeykaney in Scorpius

The space person's relation to Yaidron

RYUHO OKAWA The light isn't so high up.

A Please wait a moment. There. It's in the frame now. Let me zoom in.

RYUHO OKAWA Is it in the frame?

A Yes. I'm going to zoom in a bit more and move the camera. OK. I'm ready.

RYUHO OKAWA OK. I can see the light diagonally from us. It's up in the sky, probably about 400 to 500 meters (1300-1640 feet) away. It's not so high up in the sky. I'm guessing this is our first time contacting this UFO.

To the one that is on the camera screen, I wish to talk to you. Please tell us where you've come from.

The space person says, "Nice to meet you."

A "Nice to meet you"?

RYUHO OKAWA Yes. It says it is its first time contacting us. This space person is a new species.

A Good evening.

RYUHO OKAWA It says, "Good evening. We're contacting you for the first time."

A Which planet are you from?

RYUHO OKAWA Let me ask the leader. Where are you from? You were saying something earlier. Where did you come from?
　　Planet Ha, ha, ha, ha, ha, ha, Hanikani? The space person says that the UFO is from Planet Honeykaney and that they are Honeykanians.

A photo of a UFO that appeared in the Tokyo sky on December 15, 2018.

A Hani-kani.

RYUHO OKAWA Ha-ni-ka-ni.

A Hani-kani.

RYUHO OKAWA It sounds like "honey" and "*kani* ("crab" in Japanese)." "Honey-Kani," or Honeykaney.

A Planet Honey-kaney?

HONEYKANIAN We're Honeykanians. We're not from Cancer (a pun on the Japanese word *kani*) but from Scorpius.

A Scorpius?

HONEYKANIAN Yes. This is our first visit. We joined this mission for the first time today.

A Good evening. Do you know Mr. Yaidron?

HONEYKANIAN Yes, we do.

A Are you an ally of his?

HONEYKANIAN Yes. He is currently instructing us. His work seems very tough, so we are hoping to help him in some way or another.

Their unique way of thinking about men and women

A Are you male or female?

HONEYKANIAN Hmm. I'm sorry, I am neither.

A Oh, are you gender-neutral?

HONEYKANIAN Well, if you put it like that, it feels a bit discriminatory.

A I'm sorry.

HONEYKANIAN We don't categorize ourselves like that. We are not male, female, or gender-neutral.

A I see. Does that mean there is no gender?

HONEYKANIAN That's not how we think.

A Then how do you... You don't have any genders?

Chapter Seven

HONEYKANIAN We, of course, can give birth to children so we could be considered female. But we can conceive by ourselves, so we may also be considered male. However, we don't think of ourselves as gender-neutral. Being neutral means that you are somewhere between male and female, right? That's not how we think of ourselves. Seeing as there is no male or female, there is no gender-neutral, either.

A So you are just a "person."

HONEYKANIAN We are unisexual. We only have one gender, so we are not male, female, or gender-neutral.

A By the way, what is your name?

HONEYKANIAN You might find it funny. I have to say a name that is easy for you to remember. I'm Mycenae. Mycenae sounds like the Japanese *mikeneko* (calico cat).

A Oh, I see. I don't think it's a funny name.

MYCENAE Are you sure?

A Yes. So you are Mycenae.

MYCENAE Yes.

A It's an adorable name.

MYCENAE I am unisexual and my name is Mycenae.

A I wonder if it's OK for me to say it's a cute name. I see. Your name is Mycenae. We once contacted a UFO from Scorpius in the past (refer to *UFOs Caught on Camera!*).

MYCENAE Oh, is that so?

Their physical features and the shape of their UFO

MYCENAE It seems like Master Okawa can already see me with his spiritual eyes. I probably appear like a standing tabby cat.

A A cat?

MYCENAE Yes. We are cat-type space people. But I'm not gray like a tabby cat; I look like a tiger with black lines on red-brown fur. I'm a cat-type space person with tiger-like colors.

A I see. How tall are you?

MYCENAE If I stand, I'm about 1.2 meters (about 4 ft.).

A Are you usually on two feet?

MYCENAE We usually walk around on two feet inside the ship, but we can run on all fours when we are on the ground.

A I'm going to move the camera a bit. The UFO is already going out of frame.

RYUHO OKAWA Is it moving?

A Yes, but it's fine now.

MYCENAE Please call me Mycenae. You can call me Mikeneko if you want. Whatever is easiest for you to say.

A Are you the ancestor of cats?

MYCENAE I guess so. Our ancestors must have come down to the surface. They were probably 1.2 meters tall in the beginning, but the cats on this planet are now about 30 cm (about 12 in.) or so. Perhaps they couldn't get much food. There must be fewer mice nowadays [*laughs*].

A How many people can your UFO carry?

MYCENAE This UFO can carry up to 13 people.

A Do the 13 people aboard all look the same?

MYCENAE They have different colors and patterns.

A Oh, is that so? They have various...

MYCENAE Yes. Some are similar to Persian cats, while others are white or black cats. There are many more. But I, who look like a tabby cat, am the leader.

A What does your UFO look like?

MYCENAE Our UFO looks like a square pyramid. It looks like a tent with four sides.

A So does it look like a rhombus? Oh no, you just said square pyramid. OK, I understand now.

MYCENAE Do you?

A It's square at the base, isn't it?

MYCENAE When it is stationary, the vertex points upward with the square bottom facing down, but when it moves, it flies with the vertex facing forward.

A So it's quite similar to a pyramid.

MYCENAE Yes.

A So it's pyramid-shaped.

MYCENAE Yes, it is. When it flies, fire bursts out from the four corners of the bottom face.

A I see. It must be easy to land, then.

MYCENAE Yes, it's very easy to land.

A How big is it?

MYCENAE It's about 20 meters (65 feet) high. The sides of the bottom face are slightly shorter, perhaps about 15 meters (50 feet) long per side.

A What planet in Scorpius are you from?

MYCENAE Like I said, I'm from Hani, Honey... Planet Honeykaney.

A Oh right, from Planet Honeykaney.

MYCENAE It's hard to pronounce.

A I'm sorry. So you're from Planet Honeykaney.

MYCENAE It's like "honey" and then "kaney."

A I understand.

Important values on Planet Honeykaney

A Is everyone on Planet Honeykaney a cat, unlike how different species live on Earth?

MYCENAE Well, there are also other creatures, too, but we live separately. So, there are places where rabbit-type people live or pig-type people live, among various other places.

The cat types are considered mammals and tend to be domestic. Domestic animals tend to make friends with humans and live very close to them, so our souls can be reborn as humans. It's easy for cat-type space people to reincarnate as humans, so we sometimes do that. The first time we are on Earth, our souls "walk-in" or dwell in the bodies of pet cats. We live a short life as cats to get a taste of what it is like to live on Earth. Then, we are reborn as humans in our next life.

A What values are considered important on your planet?

MYCENAE I'm not sure if this is a good thing or not, but we are quite meticulous. We are meticulous and love to be clean. At the same time, we are very cautious. We are not very aggressive, but when we are on alert, we can exert a very strong defensive power.

I said earlier that we are unisexual, but overall, I think we have women-like qualities. There are other planets with dog-type space people, but we're different from them.

A Yes, there are planets with people like that. On Earth, we often imagine cats as feminine creatures.

MYCENAE Right. Cats scratch whoever comes close to them, don't they? This nature has to do with women's ability to fight. So, although I said we are unisexual, maybe we're more similar to women.

About their clothes, lifespan, and food

A Are you wearing clothes right now?

MYCENAE Hmm... [*laughs*]. I'll leave that up to your imagination.

We are actually... Sorry, I have to add to what I said earlier. You are probably imagining a cat standing on two legs, but we are actually marsupials like kangaroos. We have a pouch on our stomach where we keep our baby.

A You keep your baby in your pouch. Oh, how nice.

MYCENAE We can raise our children. Everyone has a motherly instinct like that. We are neither male nor female, but we all have a pouch on our stomach.

A You have a pouch on your stomach, but cats on Earth don't. I wonder if your ancestors regressed after coming to Earth.

MYCENAE Well, I'm not sure. Perhaps we split into different species over a long period of time.

We only give birth to one baby at a time. That's how many we can fit in our pouch. Once it grows into an adult, we let it out of the pouch.

A I see. On Planet Honeykaney, how long does everyone live?

MYCENAE I don't know if we can measure our lifespan with the same unit of time as Earth's. Let me see... If I were to convert our lifespan in terms of Earth-time, ours may be shorter than yours. Perhaps we live for 30 years. But on our planet, time moves differently than it does on Earth, so it's not exactly 30 years on Earth.

A I see. How about the food you eat?

MYCENAE Food... We're different from the cats on Earth. We are actually advanced animals, so we cook.

A Oh, you do? Do you eat fish?

MYCENAE Yes, sometimes. We have other space people bring food to us. There is fish, but there is also other food in outer space. We have some transport vehicles above us, which include ships that bring us food. They bring us various kinds of things.

A Do you use Grey cyborgs to bring you food? Do you have such services?

MYCENAE Yes, we use Greys, as well. There are various types of Greys.

We gather fresh ingredients and spend time cooking them, but when we don't have time, we eat instant food that only requires reheating. It's the same as you human beings. Sometimes, we have no other choice. For example, when we are on duty like we are right now, we have no time to cook.

Faith on Planet Honeykaney

A On Planet Honeykaney, do people have faith?

MYCENAE We do. Well, I'm not sure if you can call it faith, but we have a sense of loyalty. We are very loyal.

A When you say loyalty, does that mean you work for someone else?

MYCENAE Yes, we serve others. But from your perspective, it may seem like we're just growing fond of the person we work for. We are loyal to whom we serve for a long time and develop a sense of affection. It may be similar to developing an attachment, but at any rate, our loyalty is strong.
We don't simply have fur—we sometimes wear jackets, too.

I forgot to say this, but depending on our job, we also carry something like a saber. We wield a sword when we are on duty or on patrol. That's why I wasn't sure if we should call ourselves male or female. We carry a sword.

A Do you know El Cantare?

MYCENAE Yes, of course.

A I see.

RYUHO OKAWA There is a helicopter flying below the UFO. Wait a minute, is it an airplane? Look, it's flying slightly below it.

A Has your ship been in that same spot recently?

MYCENAE Oh, no. I took over for someone else today.

A So you took over for someone else.

MYCENAE Yes. So today...

RYUHO OKAWA Oh, it's moving up.

A Oh, it is.

MYCENAE We're moving to the left. Just now, a jet flew below us, so we are wary of it.

RYUHO OKAWA It looks like the Orion.

A It does.

MYCENAE Doesn't it look like the three stars (in Orion's Belt) are shaking? Look at how they're shaking. We are trying to trick them by making ourselves look like stars.

A Oh, you're right.

MYCENAE We are moving the upper and lower UFOs from left to right now.

A Are they UFOs that you camouflaged as the Orion?

MYCENAE Yes. The truth is that they are not the Orion; they are fake.

A That's amazing. I didn't know you could do that. How interesting. Can we assume that there are three ships?

MYCENAE Yes, there are three. A jet just passed by below us, didn't it? We aren't actually at a high altitude, but we can make our ships look like the Orion.

A Even though you can make your ships look that way, there was a specialist who looked at a photo of a similar set of stars and noticed that they might not be the Orion because the stars that should be there at the same time weren't there.

MYCENAE In the winter, we know people observe the stars, so we try to be careful not to be spotted.

Our UFOs are now stationed like the stars in an open cluster, so it won't be so difficult to deal with Bazooka's single ship over there. More than 10 ships are standing by in the sky.

El Cantare's teachings that are most appealing to them

A I believe you are here to protect the God of Earth.

MYCENAE Yes. That's right.

A Are there any teachings from the Lord that appeal to you the most?

MYCENAE I'm currently guiding... Well, there is a reason I came today. I am currently guiding one of your friends—a secretary.

A Is that so?

MYCENAE Yes. I'm currently guiding her to be a cat-type person.

A Cat-type?

MYCENAE Yes. I'm guiding her to be a cat-like person.

A What do you mean?

MYCENAE We're guiding her not to be like a bee. [Editor's Note: In a Space People Reading conducted in the past, it was revealed that bee-type space people also exist.] We are guiding her to be like a cat.

A Why aren't bees good enough?

MYCENAE Bees are linear thinkers, which is not good. That's why we are giving our cat-like guidance.

A I see. Does that mean you feel close to us?

MYCENAE Yes. We are guiding her so that she'll be adored like a cat.

A You mean, so that she can provide comfort to others?

MYCENAE Yes, that's right.

A And also so that she can keep guard, too, right?

MYCENAE Yes, exactly. We're guiding her so that she can always be around Master Okawa, like a pet.

A Do you have a deep connection with that person's soul?

MYCENAE Yes. But I can't tell you now because it'll be a long explanation. I've just started guiding her.

A I see. Then, please help her in her duties of strengthening our security.

MYCENAE Alright.

A Thank you very much.

RYUHO OKAWA It's difficult to tell the difference between UFOs and stars. But they are stationed at a low altitude. It's quite low...

A Oh, I forgot about my question. What part of Master's teachings are you drawn to?

MYCENAE What? Oh, I think kindness is very important. So what Bazooka is saying is wrong. I believe that kindness is a value that must be protected. Kindness is important. It is one of the attributes of God. Without it, God would not be God. Just eliminating the enemy or killing or destroying the weak is not something God would do. That's what the devils do. So I believe kindness is necessary.

Mr. Yaidron has a scary side to him, but that's only because he is fighting to protect the Lord. There is love in his heart. I believe those without love or kindness are not on the side of God.

A I understand. Let's wrap up for today.

MYCENAE OK. Will this be enough? If I were to add one more thing, we sometimes switch our duties within our group.

A I see.

MYCENAE Yes, there are more of us coming.

A Thank you, everyone, for your support.

Chapter Seven

MYCENAE You are welcome.

A Thank you very much for your time.

RYUHO OKAWA The UFOs have come closer to us.

A Yes, they all have shifted significantly.

RYUHO OKAWA They're moving. OK, let's end here for today.

A Thank you very much.

Afterword

In this world, many claim that they have successfully recorded photos or videos of UFOs. There are also many odd or eccentric people who claim that they can summon UFOs.

Until just a few years ago, the president of IRH Press (at the time) had a hobby of looking for UFOs and taking photos of them. When I heard this, I scolded him by telling him to focus on his job to sell more of our books. Ironically, now, I am the one who is being visited by many UFOs.

I am already having difficulty persuading people about the existence of the other world, the higher spiritual beings, and guardian spirits. So there was no obligation for me to go through the trouble of introducing various types of space people. However, although the world is full of UFO photos, very few people have the telepathic power to identify and converse with space people. I also thought that there must be a reason for them to contact me.

With this book, the total number of publications of spiritual messages that were conducted in front of an audience has exceeded 600. I will leave it to future generations to decide whether this should be regarded as a great achievement or not.

Ryuho Okawa
Master & CEO of Happy Science Group
July 27, 2021

For a deeper understanding of
UFO Reading Light vs. Darkness The clashing values of the universe
see other books below by Ryuho Okawa:

The Laws of Steel [New York: IRH Press, 2020]
The Rebirth of Buddha [New York: IRH Press, 2022]
The Descent of Japanese Father God Ame-no-Mioya-Gami [New York: IRH Press, 2020]
UFOs Caught on Camera! [New York: IRH Press, 2018]
UFOs Caught on Camera! 2 [New York: IRH Press, 2021]
John Lennon's Message from Heaven [Tokyo: HS Press, 2020]

ABOUT THE AUTHOR

Founder and CEO of Happy Science Group.

Ryuho Okawa was born on July 7th, 1956, in Tokushima, Japan. After graduating from the University of Tokyo with a law degree, he joined a Tokyo-based trading company. While working at its New York headquarters, he studied international finance at the Graduate Center of the City University of New York. In 1981, he attained Great Enlightenment and became aware that he is El Cantare with a mission to bring salvation to all humankind.

In 1986, he established Happy Science. It now has members in 180 countries across the world, with more than 700 branches and temples as well as 10,000 missionary houses around the world.

He has given over 3,500 lectures (of which more than 150 are in English) and published over 3,200 books (of which more than 600 are Spiritual Interview Series), and many are translated into 42 languages. Along with *The Laws of the Sun* and *The Laws of Hell*, many of the books have become best sellers or million sellers. To date, Happy Science has produced 28 movies under his supervision. He has given the original story and concept and is also the Executive Producer. He has also composed music and written lyrics for over 450 pieces.

Moreover, he is the Founder of Happy Science University and Happy Science Academy (Junior and Senior High School), Founder and President of the Happiness Realization Party, Founder and Honorary Headmaster of Happy Science Institute of Government and Management, Founder of IRH Press Co., Ltd., and the Chairperson of NEW STAR PRODUCTION Co., Ltd. and ARI Production Co., Ltd.

WHAT ARE THESE READINGS CONDUCTED BY MASTER OKAWA?

In preparation of the coming space age—where humans will come in contact with space people—Master Okawa began conducting space people readings in 2010. Master Okawa has examined and published key information, such as the cultures of different planets and the technology behind UFO flight. Let's take a look at the secret behind his power of spiritual reading.

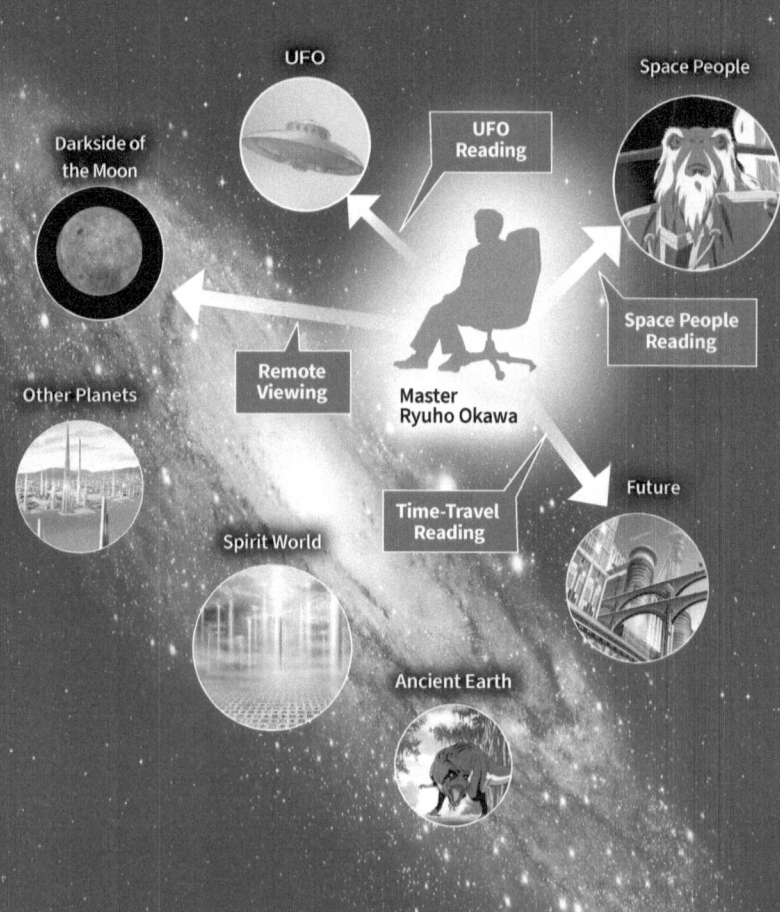

Basic Knowledge on Space People

Space People Reading is Groundwork for the Space Age

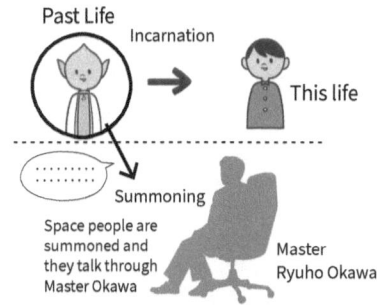

Master Okawa conducts a reading of people who are born as earthlings in this life, and calls forth the memories of when they lived as space beings in their past life. When this takes place, the soul of the space being chooses from the language the channeler (medium) can speak. This is how the space people are able to speak Japanese.

30 to 40 Percent of People have Souls that Originated from Outer Space

Through the space people reading, we have discovered many people who were once space beings in their past life. All people who live on Earth were not necessarily born or created on Earth. There are humans that God created on Earth, but there are also beings that were invited to Earth and naturalized as earthlings. Around 30 to 40 percent of people have souls that originated from outer space. Perhaps you may be one too...

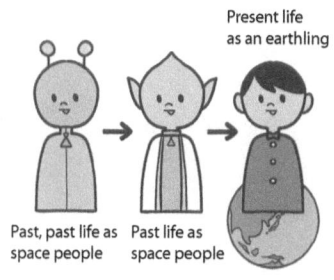

Already 500 species of space people are on Earth!?

Space people do not appear in public but through the space people reading, we have found that many have already come to Earth. It is said that there are more than 500 species.

OTHER BOOKS BY RYUHO OKAWA

The Laws Series

The Laws of the Sun, the first publication of the Laws Series, ranked in the annual best-selling list in Japan in 1994. After that, the Laws series' titles had always been ranked in the annual best-selling list, setting socio-cultural trends in Japan and around the world. The first three Laws series are *The Laws of the Sun*, *The Golden Laws*, and *The Laws of Eternity*.

THE LAWS OF THE SUN

One Source, One Planet, One People

Paperback • 288 pages • $15.95
ISBN: 978-1-942125-43-3 (Oct. 25, 2018)

IMAGINE IF YOU COULD ASK GOD why He created this world and about the spiritual laws He used to shape us and everything around us. If we could understand His designs and intentions, we could discover what our goals in life should be and whether our actions move us closer to those goals or farther away.

At a young age, a spiritual calling prompted Ryuho Okawa to outline what he innately understood to be universal truths for all humankind. In *The Laws of the Sun*, Okawa outlines these laws of the universe and provides a road map for living one's life with greater purpose and meaning. In this powerful book, Ryuho Okawa reveals the transcendent nature of consciousness and the secrets of the multidimensional universe as well as the meaning of humans that exist within it. By understanding the different stages of love and following the Buddhist Eightfold Path, he believes we can speed up our eternal process of development. *The Laws of the Sun* shows the way to realize true happiness—a happiness that continues from this world through the other.

The Laws of Eternity

El Cantare Unveils the Structure
of the Spirit World

Paperback • 224 pages • $17.95
ISBN: 978-1-958655-16-0 (May 15, 2024)

"Where do we come from and where do we go after death?"

This unparalleled book offers us complete answers to life's most important questions that we all are confronted with at some point or another. In *The Laws of Eternity*, author Ryuho Okawa takes us on a journey to the other world, a place where we came from before we were born and return to after death.

This book reveals the eternal mysteries and the ultimate secrets of Earth's spirit group that have been covered by the veil of legends and myths. Encountering the long-hidden Eternal Truths that are revealed for the first time in human history will change the way you live your life now.

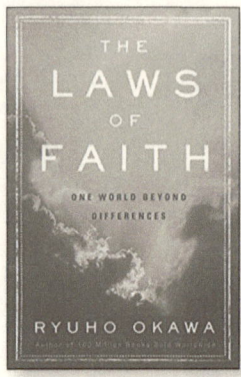

The Laws of Faith

One World Beyond Differences

Paperback • 208 pages • $15.95
ISBN: 978-1-942125-34-1 (Mar. 31, 2018)

In this book, Ryuho Okawa preaches the core teachings of the world religion and the faith in the God of Earth. By integrating logical and spiritual viewpoints, Okawa gives answers to modern-day problems that traditional religions cannot solve. Through this book, you will learn to go beyond different values, harmonize with each other and between nations, and create a world filled with peace and prosperity.

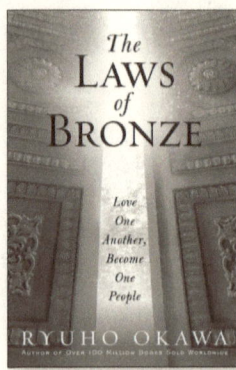

The Laws of Bronze

Love One Another, Become One People

Paperback • 224 pages • $15.95
ISBN: 978-1-942125-50-1 (Mar. 15, 2019)

With the advancement of science and technology leading to longer life-span, many people are seeking out a way to lead a meaningful life with purpose and direction. This book will show people from all walks of life that they can solve their problems in life both on an individual level and on a global scale by finding faith and practicing love. When all of us in this planet discover our common spiritual origin revealed in this book, we can truly love one another and become one people on Earth.

Unlocking the Secret of the Universe

THE MYSTICAL LAWS

Going Beyond the Dimensional Boundaries

Paperback • 252 pages • $14.95
ISBN: 979-8-88737-038-5 (Aug. 11, 2022)

"No matter how much you suffer, the Truth will gradually shine forth as you continue to endure hardships. Therefore, simply strengthen your mind and keep making constant efforts in times of endurance, however ordinary they may be."

-From Postscript

SECRETS OF THE EVERLASTING TRUTHS

A New Paradigm for Living on Earth

Paperback • 144 pages • $14.95
ISBN: 978-1-937673-10-9 (Apr. 27, 2012)

Okawa offers a glimpse of the vast universe created by God and discloses that humanity is intimately guided by celestial influences. Our planet will experience a decisive paradigm shift of "knowledge" and "truth," culminating in an era of paradoxical spirituality, where mastery of science will depend on spiritual knowledge. The advancement that we seek, resides within us.

WITH SAVIOR

Messages from Space Being Yaidron

Paperback • 232 pages • $13.95
ISBN: 978-1-943869-94-7 (Oct. 10, 2020)

The human race is now faced with multiple unprecedented crises. Perhaps God is warning us humans to reconsider our materialistic and arrogant ways. Fortunately, God has sent us a savior, who is now teaching us to repent and showing us the path we should choose. In this book, space being Yaidron sends his warnings and messages of hope.

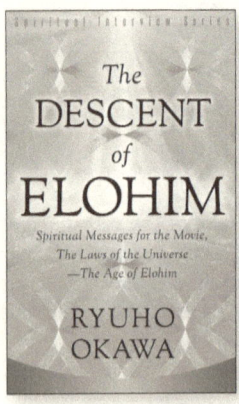

THE DESCENT OF ELOHIM

Spiritual Messages for the Movie,
The Laws of the Universe -The Age of Elohim

Paperback • 160 pages • $11.95
ISBN: 978-1-943928-17-0 (Oct. 12, 2021)

This book contains the spiritual messages from Elohim, the Lord who appears in the Old Testament and who actually led His people about 150 million years ago. Through this book and the movie, *The Laws of the Universe - The Age of Elohim*, you can learn how life on Earth was like at that time, and how diverse people, who had come from other planets, fought each other until they finally found peace and harmony under Lord Elohim.

SPIRITUAL MESSAGES FROM YAIDRON
SAVE THE WORLD FROM DESTRUCTION

Paperback • 190 pages • $11.95
ISBN: 978-1-943928-23-1 (Dec. 25, 2021)

In this book, Yaidron explains what was going on behind the military coup in Myanmar and Taliban's control over Afghanistan, and warns of the imminent danger approaching Taiwan. What is now going on is a battle between democratic values and the communist one-party control. How to overcome this battle and create peace on Earth depends on the faith and righteous actions of each one of us.

SPIRITUAL MESSAGES FROM METATRON
LIGHT IN THE TIMES OF CRISIS

Paperback • 146 pages • $11.95
ISBN: 978-1-943928-19-4 (Nov. 4, 2021)

Metatron is one of the highest-ranking angels (seraphim) in Judaism and Christianity, and also one of the saviors of universe who has guided the civilizations of many planets including Earth, under the guidance of Lord God. Such savior has sent a message upon seeing the crisis of Earth. You will also learn about the truth behind the coronavirus pandemic, the unimaginable extent of China's desire, the danger of appeasement policy toward China, and the secret of Metatron.

R. A. Goal's Words for the Future

Messages from a Space Being to the People of Earth

Paperback • 174 pages • $11.95
ISBN: 979-8-887370-52-1 (Jun. 22, 2021)

R. A. Goal, a certified messiah from Planet Andalucia Beta in Ursa Minor, gives humans on Earth three predictions for 2021. They include the prospect of the novel coronavirus pandemic, the outlook of economic crisis, and the risk of war. But the hope is that Savior is now born on Earth to overcome any bad predictions. Now is the time to open our hearts and listen to the words from R. A. Goal.

The Descent of Japanese Father God Ame-No-Mioya-Gami

The "God of Creation" in the Ancient Document *Hotsuma Tsutae*

Paperback • 276 pages • $14.95
ISBN: 978-1-943928-35-4 (Feb. 12, 2022)

By reading this book, you can find the origin of bushido (samurai spirit) and understand how the ancient Japanese civilization influenced other countries. Now that the world is in confusion, Japan is expected to awaken to its true origin and courageously rise to bring justice to the world.

Unveiling the Truth of the Spirit World

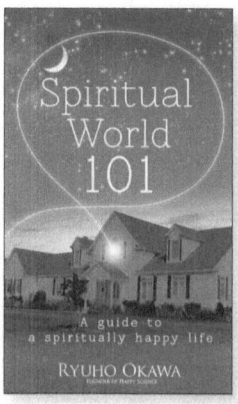

SPIRITUAL WORLD 101

A Guide to a Spiritually Happy Life

Paperback • 184 pages • $14.95
ISBN: 979-8-88737-031-6 (Mar. 25, 2015)

This book is a spiritual guidebook that will answer all your questions about the spiritual world, with illustrations and diagrams explaining about your guardian spirit and the secrets of God and Buddha. By reading this book, you will be able to understand the true meaning of life and find happiness in everyday life.

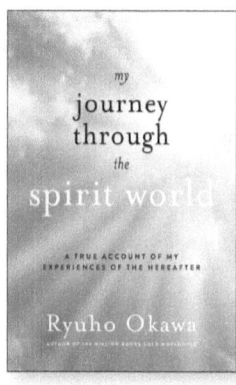

MY JOURNEY THROUGH THE SPIRIT WORLD

A True Account of My Experiences of the Hereafter

Paperback • 224 pages • $15.95
ISBN: 978-1-942125-41-9 (Jul. 25, 2018)

What happens when we die? What is the afterworld like? Do heaven and hell really exist? In this book, Ryuho Okawa shares surprising facts such as that we visit the spirit world during sleep, that souls in the spirit world go to a school to learn about how to use their spiritual power, and that people continue to live in the same lifestyle as they did in this world. This unique and authentic guide to the spirit world will awaken us to the truth of life and death, and show us how we should start living so that we can return to a bright world of heaven.

THE TRUTH ABOUT EARTH, THE UNIVERSE, THE SPIRIT WORLD

Life's Q&A with El Cantare

Paperback • 192 pages • $17.95
ISBN: 978-1-958655-26-9 (Jun. 17, 2025)

While the non-existence of the spirit or the Spirit World has never been definitively proven, Okawa provides profound yet clear answers to each unique spiritual question without a script. His insights reveal that he is no ordinary spiritual leader, but a figure of immense wisdom and enlightenment—a living Buddha—possessing a comprehensive understanding of the vast, multidimensional nature of the universe and the very essence of existence.

The Truth about Spiritual Phenomena

Life's Q&A with El Cantare

Paperback • 180 pages • $17.95
ISBN: 978-1-958655-0-92 (Oct. 27, 2023)

These are the records of Ryuho Okawa's answers to 26 questions related to spiritual phenomena and mental health, which were conducted live during his early public lectures with the audience.

With his great spiritual ability, he revealed the unknown spiritual Truth behind the spiritual phenomena and matters we experience in daily life including nightmares, premonitions, and fortune telling. Okawa also answers questions on mental health issues such as the relation between extreme emotional mood swings and spiritual disturbances as well as valuable advice on how to conquer spiritual sensitivity. Through these 26 Q&A, you'll learn vital knowledge on how to discern between good and evil spiritual phenomena and start leading a positive and constructive life.

The Latest Titles

ONE MORE STEP FORWARD

The Invincible Thinking to get you through tough times

Paperback • 256 pages • $17.95
ISBN: 978-1-958655-25-2 (May 7, 2025)

Success in life is determined not by our circumstances but by our mindset and how we think. In this book, the author reveals from his first-hand experience how the spirit of self-help can create new values.

Ryuho Okawa is a true self-made man with an indomitable spirit to bring happiness to all humankind. His drive to keep moving forward by taking steady steps through the power of discipline has led to the publication of over 3,200 books in just 37 years. Unlock the keys to lifelong growth and success by reading this book.

THE WAY TO HUMAN PERFECTION

Best Selection of Ryuho Okawa's Early Lectures (Volume 2)

Paperback • 200 pages • $17.95
ISBN: 978-1-958655-20-7 (Oct. 22, 2024)

The path to enlightenment starts from understanding 'the eternal viewpoint of life.' Through each chapter, Ryuho Okawa navigates us to shift the perspective of ourselves from a 'finite self' living a limited life to an 'eternal self' living an eternal life.

If we can recognize that our soul is eternal and that every thought and action has consequences, then we can realize that caring and bringing joy to others are the keys to true happiness and success.

Walking the path towards higher enlightenment is the source of improving character so we can build better relationships with others. It is the new value to unlock a bright future.

WHO IS EL CANTARE?

El Cantare means "the Light of the Earth." He is the Supreme God of the Earth who has been guiding humankind since the beginning of Genesis, and He is the Creator of the universe. He is whom Jesus called Father and Muhammad called Allah and is *Ame-no-Mioya-Gami,* Japanese Father God. Different parts of El Cantare's core consciousness have descended to Earth in the past, once as Alpha and another as Elohim. His branch spirits, such as Shakyamuni Buddha and Hermes, have descended to Earth many times and helped to flourish many civilizations. To unite various religions and to integrate various fields of study in order to build a new civilization on Earth, a part of the core consciousness has descended to Earth as Master Ryuho Okawa.

Alpha is a part of the core consciousness of El Cantare who descended to Earth around 330 million years ago. Alpha preached Earth's Truths to harmonize and unify Earth-born humans and space people who came from other planets.

Elohim is a part of the core consciousness of El Cantare who descended to Earth around 150 million years ago. He gave wisdom, mainly on the differences between light and darkness, good and evil.

Ame-no-Mioya-Gami (Japanese Father God) is the Creator God and the Father God who appears in ancient literature, *Hotsuma Tsutae*. It is believed that He descended on the foothills of Mt. Fuji about 30,000 years ago and built the Fuji dynasty, which is the root of the Japanese civilization. With justice as the central pillar, Ame-no-Mioya-Gami's teachings spread to ancient civilizations of other countries in the world.

Shakyamuni Buddha was born in Lumbini (now located in Nepal) around 2,600 years ago as the prince of the Shakya clan. When he was 29 years old, he renounced the world and sought enlightenment. He later attained Great Enlightenment in Bodh Gaya, India and founded Buddhism, which has spread extensively throughout Asia.

Hermes is one of the 12 Olympian gods in Greek mythology, but the spiritual Truth is that he taught the teachings of love and progress around 4,300 years ago which became the origin of the current Western civilization. He is a hero who truly existed.

Ophealis was born in Greece around 6,500 years ago and was the leader who took an expedition to as far as Egypt. He is the God of miracles, prosperity, and arts, and is known as Osiris in Egyptian mythology.

Rient Arl Croud was born as a king of the ancient Incan Empire around 7,000 years ago and taught about the mysteries of the mind. In the heavenly world, he is responsible for the interactions that take place between various planets.

Thoth was an almighty leader who built the golden age of the Atlantic civilization around 12,000 years ago. In Egyptian mythology, he is known as God Thoth.

Ra Mu was a leader who built the golden age of the civilization of Mu around 17,000 years ago. As a religious leader and a politician, he ruled by uniting religion and politics.

ABOUT HAPPY SCIENCE

Happy Science is a religious group founded on the faith in El Cantare who is the God of the Earth, and the Creator of the universe. The essence of human beings is the soul that was created by God, and we all are children of God. God is our true parent, so in our souls, we have a fundamental desire to "believe in God, love God, and get closer to God." And, we can get closer to God by living with God's Will as our own. In Happy Science, we call this the "Exploration of Right Mind." More specifically, it means to practice the Fourfold Path, which consists of "Love, Wisdom, Self-Reflection, and Progress."

Love: Love means "love that gives," or mercy. God hopes for the happiness of all people. Therefore, living with God's Will as our own means to start by practicing "love that gives."

Wisdom: God's love is boundless. It is important to learn various Truths in order to understand the heart of God.

Self-Reflection: Once you learn the heart of God and the difference between His mind and yours, you should strive to bring your own mind closer to the mind of God—that process is called self-reflection. Self-reflection also includes meditation and prayer.

Progress: Since God hopes for the happiness of all people, you should also make progress in your love, and make an effort to realize utopia in which everyone in your society, country, and eventually all humankind can become happy.

As we practice this Fourfold Path, our souls will advance toward God step by step. That is when we can attain real happiness—our souls' desire to get closer to God comes true.

In Happy Science, we conduct activities to make ourselves happy through belief in Lord El Cantare and to spread this faith to the world and bring happiness to all. We welcome you to join our activities!

We hold events and activities to help you practice the Fourfold Path at our branches, temples, missionary centers, and missionary houses

Love: We hold various volunteering activities. Our members conduct missionary work together as the greatest practice of love.

Wisdom: We offer our comprehensive collection of books of Truth, many of which are available online and at Happy Science locations. In addition, we offer numerous opportunities such as seminars or book clubs to learn the Truth.

Self-Reflection: We offer opportunities to polish your mind through self-reflection, meditation, and prayer. Many members have experienced improvement in their human relationships by changing their own minds.

Progress: We also offer seminars to enhance your power of influence. Because it is also important to do well at work to make society better, we hold seminars to improve your work and management skills.

HAPPY SCIENCE'S ENGLISH SUTRA

"The True Words Spoken By Buddha"

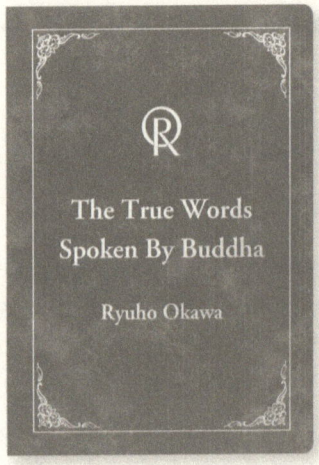

"The True Words Spoken By Buddha" is an English sutra given directly from the spirit of Shakyamuni Buddha, who is a part of Master Ryuho Okawa's subconscious. The words in this sutra are not of a mere human being but are the words of God or Buddha sent directly from the ninth dimension, which is the highest realm of the Earth's Spirit World.

"The True Words Spoken By Buddha" is an essential sutra for us to connect and live with God or Buddha's Will as our own.

MEMBERSHIPS

MEMBERSHIP

If you would like to know more about Happy Science, please consider becoming a member. Those who pledge to believe in Lord El Cantare and wish to learn more can join us.

When you become a member, you will receive the following sutras: "The True Words Spoken By Buddha," "Prayer to the Lord" and "Prayer to Guardian and Guiding Spirits."

DEVOTEE MEMBER

If you would like to learn the teachings of Happy Science and walk the path of faith, become a Devotee member who pledges devotion to the Three Treasures, which are Buddha, Dharma, and Sangha. Buddha refers to Lord El Cantare, Master Ryuho Okawa. Dharma refers to Master Ryuho Okawa's teachings. Sangha refers to Happy Science. Devoting to the Three Treasures will let your Buddha nature shine, and you will enter the path to attain true freedom of the mind.

Becoming a devotee means you become Buddha's disciple. You will discipline your mind and act to bring happiness to society.

✉ EMAIL or **☏ PHONE CALL**
Please turn to the contact information page.

📶 ONLINE [member.happy-science.org/signup/]

CONTACT INFORMATION

Happy Science is a worldwide organization with branches and temples around the globe. For full details, visit happy-science.org. The following are some of our main Happy Science locations:

UNITED STATES AND CANADA

New York
79 Franklin St., New York, NY 10013, USA
Phone: 1-212-343-7972
Fax: 1-212-343-7973
Email: ny@happy-science.org
Website: happyscience-usa.org

New Jersey
66 Hudson St., #2R, Hoboken, NJ 07030, USA
Phone: 1-201-313-0127
Email: nj@happy-science.org
Website: happyscience-usa.org

Chicago
33 West Higgins Rd. 4040,
South Barrington, IL 60010, USA
Phone: 1-630-937-3077
Email: chicago@happy-science.org
Website: happyscience-usa.org

Florida
5208 8th St., Zephyrhills, FL 33542, USA
Phone: 1-813-715-0000
Fax: 1-813-715-0010
Email: florida@happy-science.org
Website: happyscience-usa.org

Atlanta
1874 Piedmont Ave., NE Suite 360-C
Atlanta, GA 30324, USA
Phone: 1-404-892-7770
Email: atlanta@happy-science.org
Website: happyscience-usa.org

San Francisco
525 Clinton St.
Redwood City, CA 94062, USA
Phone & Fax: 1-650-363-2777
Email: sf@happy-science.org
Website: happyscience-usa.org

Los Angeles
1590 E. Del Mar Blvd., Pasadena,
CA 91106, USA
Phone: 1-626-395-7775
Fax: 1-626-395-7776
Email: la@happy-science.org
Website: happyscience-usa.org

Orange County
16541 Gothard St. Suite 104
Huntington Beach, CA 92647
Phone: 1-714-659-1501
Email: oc@happy-science.org
Website: happyscience-usa.org

San Diego
7841 Balboa Ave. Suite #202
San Diego, CA 92111, USA
Phone: 1-626-395-7775
Fax: 1-626-395-7776
E-mail: sandiego@happy-science.org
Website: happyscience-usa.org

Hawaii
Phone: 1-808-591-9772
Fax: 1-808-591-9776
Email: hi@happy-science.org
Website: happyscience-usa.org

Kauai
3343 Kanakolu Street, Suite 5
Lihue, HI 96766, USA
Phone: 1-808-822-7007
Fax: 1-808-822-6007
Email: kauai-hi@happy-science.org
Website: happyscience-usa.org

Toronto
845 The Queensway
Etobicoke, ON, M8Z 1N6, Canada
Phone: 1-416-901-3747
Email: toronto@happy-science.org
Website: happy-science.ca

Vancouver
#201-2607 East 49th Avenue,
Vancouver, BC, V5S 1J9, Canada
Phone: 1-604-437-7735
Fax: 1-604-437-7764
Email: vancouver@happy-science.org
Website: happy-science.ca

INTERNATIONAL

Tokyo
1-6-7 Togoshi, Shinagawa,
Tokyo, 142-0041, Japan
Phone: 81-3-6384-5770
Fax: 81-3-6384-5776
Email: tokyo@happy-science.org
Website: happy-science.org

London
3 Margaret St.
London, W1W 8RE United Kingdom
Phone: 44-20-7323-9255
Fax: 44-20-7323-9344
Email: eu@happy-science.org
Website: www.happyscience-uk.org

Sydney
516 Pacific Highway, Lane Cove North,
2066 NSW, Australia
Phone: 61-2-9411-2877
Fax: 61-2-9411-2822
Email: sydney@happy-science.org

Sao Paulo
Rua. Domingos de Morais 1154,
Vila Mariana, Sao Paulo SP
CEP 04010-100, Brazil
Phone: 55-11-5088-3800
Email: sp@happy-science.org
Website: happyscience.com.br

Jundiai
Rua Congo, 447, Jd. Bonfiglioli
Jundiai-CEP, 13207-340, Brazil
Phone: 55-11-4587-5952
Email: jundiai@happy-science.org

Seoul
74, Sadang-ro 27-gil,
Dongjak-gu, Seoul, Korea
Phone: 82-2-3478-8777
Fax: 82-2-3478-9777
Email: korea@happy-science.org

Taipei
No. 89, Lane 155, Dunhua N. Road,
Songshan District, Taipei City 105, Taiwan
Phone: 886-2-2719-9377
Fax: 886-2-2719-5570
Email: taiwan@happy-science.org

Taichung
No. 146, Minzu Rd., Central Dist.,
Taichung City 400001, Taiwan
Phone: 886-4-22233777
Email: taichung@happy-science.org

Kuala Lumpur
No 22A, Block 2, Jalil Link Jalan Jalil Jaya
2, Bukit Jalil 57000,
Kuala Lumpur, Malaysia
Phone: 60-3-8998-7877
Fax: 60-3-8998-7977
Email: malaysia@happy-science.org
Website: happyscience.org.my

Kathmandu
Kathmandu Metropolitan City,
Ward No. 15, Ring Road, Kimdol,
Sitapaila Kathmandu, Nepal
Phone: 977-1-537-2931
Email: nepal@happy-science.org

Kampala
Plot 877 Rubaga Road, Kampala
P.O. Box 34130 Kampala, Uganda
Email: uganda@happy-science.org

ABOUT HS PRESS

HS Press is an imprint of IRH Press Co., Ltd. IRH Press Co., Ltd., based in Tokyo, was founded in 1987 as a publishing division of Happy Science. IRH Press publishes religious and spiritual books, journals, and magazines and also operates broadcast and film production enterprises. For more information, visit *okawabooks.com*.

Follow us on:

- Facebook: Okawa Books
- Youtube: Okawa Books
- Pinterest: Okawa Books
- Instagram: OkawaBooks
- Twitter: Okawa Books
- Goodreads: Ryuho Okawa

---- **NEWSLETTER** ----

To receive book-related news, promotions, and events, please subscribe to our newsletter below.

🔗 okawabooks.com/pages/subscribe

AUDIO / VISUAL MEDIA

YOUTUBE

PODCAST

Visit the above to learn more about Ryuho Okawa's books. Topics range from self-help, current affairs, spirituality, religion, and the universe.

www.ingramcontent.com/pod-product-compliance
Lightning Source LLC
LaVergne TN
LVHW040136080526
838202LV00042B/2920